HOME COOKING WITH
CHARLIE TROTTER

HOME COOKING WITH
CHARLIE TROTTER

by Charlie Trotter

photography by Kipling Swehla

TEN SPEED PRESS
Berkeley | Toronto

Ten Speed Press
PO Box 7123
Berkeley, California 94707
www.tenspeed.com

Distributed in Australia by Simon and Schuster Australia, in Canada by Ten Speed Press Canada, in
New Zealand by Southern Publishers Group, in South Africa by Real Books, in Southeast Asia by
Berkeley Books, and in the United Kingdom and Europe by Airlift Book Company.

Designers: Nancy Austin and Katy Brown
Project Managers: Judi Carle, Rochelle Smith
Ten Speed Press editors: Aaron Wehner, Melissa Moore
Copyeditor: Suzanne Sherman
Proofreaders: Sharon Silva, Leslie Evans
Recipe testing: Sari Zernich, Rochelle Smith
Research and recipe development: Sari Zernich, Matthias Merges

Library of Congress Cataloging-in-Publication Data

Trotter, Charlie.
   Home cooking with Charlie Trotter / by Charlie Trotter ; photography by Kipling Swehla.
      p. cm.
   Previously published under title: Charlie Trotter cooks at home.
   "Presents more than 130 recipes that make Charlie Trotter's food accessible to home cooks, with
new photography and an updated design accompanying approachable recipes for Trotter's award-
winning cuisine."—Provided by publisher.
   Includes index.
   ISBN 978-1-58008-934-0
   1. Cookery. 2. Charlie Trotter's (Restaurant) I. Trotter, Charlie. Charlie Trotter cooks at home.
   II. Title.
   TX714.T7695 2008
   641.5—dc22

                                        2008013090
First printing this edition, 2008
Printed in China

1 2 3 4 5 6 7 8 9 10 — 12 11 10 09 08

contents

introduction   1

the basics   2

planning a menu   7

pairing food and wine   8

sample menus   9

STARTERS   17

appetizers   18

soups   39

salads   54

ENTRÉES   73

seafood   74

poultry   105

meat   121

vegetables   149

DESSERTS   165

soups, sorbets, and granités   166

tarts, pies, and pastries   176

cakes, custards, and puddings   196

introduction

IT'S A CHALLENGE TO OPERATE a busy 100-seat restaurant and create new dishes each day that will inspire diners. At Charlie Trotter's, guests expect a bit of magic in every course delivered to the table. Fortunately, my job is made easier by the network of specialty food purveyors with whom I have long-standing relationships. Organic lamb from Wisconsin, truffles from the French and Italian countryside, morels from Michigan's Upper Peninsula, and ramps from the wilds of Virginia's Shenandoah Valley are only a phone call away.

While grocery stores across the country are expanding their offerings in response to the increased sophistication of shoppers, the home cook's access to gourmet ingredients—especially in rural areas—can still be limited. The time constraints of a demanding job and raising a family can pose further challenges, making it difficult for home cooks to orchestrate complex multicourse meals. Great food doesn't have to entail frantic foraging for ingredients and performing Herculean feats in the kitchen, however. With a few basic foodstuffs and a touch of bravado, home cooks can create flavorful dishes that will impress even the most ardent gourmet.

The recipes in this book were created with just such a goal in mind—elevating everyday cuisine to a higher level of sophistication. The ingredient lists are necessarily simple in scope, yet I believe you'll find the resulting dishes flavorful and well worth making time and again. While you may come across the odd ingredient you aren't familiar with—say, Korea's ubiquitous table condiment, kimchi, or Japan's fiery togarashi spice blend—you may be surprised that your local store stocks it. If you don't have access to gourmet specialty stores or Asian markets, or you simply don't have time, try shopping on the Internet. There are many excellent gourmet food e-commerce sites that will ship directly to your door. And, best of all, they are open twenty-four hours a day. When you are experimenting with recipes throughout the book, don't hesitate to mix and match elements from different recipes to suit your tastes and the ingredients available. Our menu at the restaurant evolves out of just such spontaneity, guided by basic considerations of taste and texture. In planning your meals, take your cue from the seasons—what looks best on the market stand is likely to taste best when it reaches the table.

The Basics

Great cooking has always been about great ingredients. That holds true for the sauces and accompaniments as well as for the main ingredients. Although all of the recipes that follow are items that could be purchased at the grocery store, I cannot stress enough the importance of making these foods from scratch. There is no comparison between canned and homemade stocks or store-bought roasted red bell peppers packed in oil and freshly roasted red bell peppers. The homemade version will always be more flavorful, it will be seasoned to your taste, and it won't contain preservatives or emulsifiers.

STOCKS

Stocks are the building blocks of cuisine. At the restaurant, we use some type of stock or reduction to prepare almost every dish. Stocks are extremely versatile and can add a vast range of flavors to your cooking. They can be infused with herbs or spices, reduced down to any thickness, or used as bases for soups. Stocks can also be used in place of water to add a wonderful richness and depth of flavor to dried beans, lentils, and grains.

Making stocks and reduction sauces may seem like a time-consuming proposition, but they really require very little preparation time. Once they are simmering, they simply need to be skimmed every hour or two. In one or two Sunday afternoons you can make enough stocks and reduction sauces to last for several months. They can be frozen in ice-cube trays, popped out in frozen cubes, and stored in plastic bags in the freezer for several months.

There are five rules to follow when making stocks and reductions:

- Always use cold liquid. Hot water causes the protein and fat released from the meat to emulsify, which makes the stock cloudy.

- Don't use too much liquid. The higher the proportion of solid ingredients to liquid, the more flavorful the stock will be.

- Never allow a stock to boil. Boiling emulsifies the protein and fat, whereas simmering allows the impurities to rise to the surface where they can easily be skimmed off and discarded.

- Don't stir the stock after it starts to simmer. Stirring emulsifies the protein and fat.

- When straining finished stocks, allow enough time for the liquid to drain naturally, and do not press on the ingredients in the sieve.

Once you experience the new dimension the following stocks can bring to your cooking, they will become a permanent fixture in your freezer.

Meat Stock

YIELD: 2 QUARTS

6 pounds meat bones (beef, lamb, venison, or veal)

2 cups chopped carrots

2 cups chopped celery

4 cups chopped yellow onions

3 cloves garlic, peeled

2 tablespoons canola oil

$1/2$ cup chopped tomato

2 cups red wine

1 bay leaf

1 tablespoon black peppercorns

PREHEAT the oven to 450°. Place the bones in a large roasting pan and roast for 1 hour, or until golden brown, turning the bones after 30 minutes to ensure even browning.

COOK the carrots, celery, onions, and garlic with the canola oil in a large stockpot over medium-high heat for 7 to 10 minutes, or until caramelized. Add the tomato and cook for 2 minutes. Add the red wine and cook for 15 minutes, or until most of the wine has cooked out. Add the browned bones, bay leaf, and peppercorns and cover with cold water. Bring to a boil and then decrease to low heat. Simmer slowly for 6 to 8 hours, or until reduced to 2 quarts, skimming every 30 minutes to remove the impurities that rise to the surface. Strain the stock through a fine-mesh sieve and use as desired.

Meat Stock Reduction

YIELD: 2 CUPS

2 cups chopped yellow onions

1 cup chopped carrots

1 cup chopped celery

2 tablespoons canola oil

1 cup red wine

2 quarts meat stock (see page 3)

4 sprigs thyme

COOK the onions, carrots, and celery with the canola oil in a large saucepan over medium-high heat for 10 minutes, or until golden brown. Add the red wine and cook for 10 minutes, or until most of the wine has cooked out. Add the stock, decrease the heat, and simmer over low heat for 1 hour. Strain, return to the saucepan, add the thyme, and simmer for 5 minutes. Remove the thyme and simmer for 30 minutes, or until reduced to 2 cups. Strain through a fine-mesh sieve and use as desired.

Chicken Stock

YIELD: 2 QUARTS

6 pounds chicken bones

3 cups chopped yellow onions

2 cups chopped carrots

2 cups chopped celery

1 cup chopped leeks

1 tablespoon whole white peppercorns

1 bay leaf

PLACE all of the ingredients in a large stockpot and cover three-quarters of the way with cold water. Bring to a boil, decrease the heat, and simmer slowly over low heat for 4 hours, skimming every 30 minutes to remove the impurities that rise to the surface. Strain through a fine-mesh sieve and cook over low heat for 30 to 45 minutes, or until reduced to 2 quarts. Use as desired.

Vegetable Stock

YIELD: 2 QUARTS

4 large yellow onions, chopped

6 stalks celery, coarsely chopped

1 celery root, peeled and coarsely chopped

2 carrots, peeled and coarsely chopped

2 red bell peppers, seeded, deribbed, and coarsely chopped

1 rutabaga, peeled and coarsely chopped

1 bulb fennel, peeled and coarsely chopped

2 parsnips, peeled and coarsely chopped

2 bulbs garlic, halved

1 tablespoon black peppercorns

PLACE all of the ingredients in a large stockpot and cover with cold water. Bring to a boil, decrease the heat, and simmer slowly over low heat for 1 hour. Strain through a fine-mesh sieve and cook over medium heat for 30 to 45 minutes, or until reduced to about 2 quarts. Use as desired.

THE GOURMET PANTRY

Like the stocks, the following recipes are the building blocks of great dishes. Different from the stocks, however, these foods should never be frozen for later use. Freezing causes textural and flavor changes that will affect the outcome of a dish. But all of these recipes can be prepared ahead to make the preparation of a dish simpler.

Roasted Bell Pepper

YIELD: 1 PEPPER

1 red or yellow bell pepper
(or substitute a chile pepper variety)

2 teaspoons olive oil

COAT the pepper with the olive oil. Place on an open grill or flame on the stovetop and roast, turning occasionally, for 10 minutes, or until the pepper is completely blackened. Place the roasted pepper in a small bowl, cover with plastic wrap, and let stand for 5 minutes. Peel off the skin and seed the peppers. Use immediately, or wrap tightly in plastic wrap and refrigerate for up to 1 day.

Roasted Garlic

YIELD: ABOUT 3/4 CUP

4 bulbs garlic, tops cut off

3 cups milk

1/2 cup olive oil

PREHEAT the oven to 350°. Place the garlic in a small saucepan, cover with the milk, and simmer over low heat for 10 minutes. Drain the milk and discard, place the garlic bulbs, bottom side down, in an ovenproof pan, add the olive oil, and cover. Bake for 1 to 1$^1/_2$ hours, or until the bulbs are soft. Cool the garlic in the oil and then squeeze the soft garlic cloves out of the skins. Use immediately, or refrigerate in the oil for up to 3 days.

Roasted Mushrooms

YIELD: ABOUT 2 CUPS

2$^1/_2$ cups cleaned and stemmed mushrooms
(such as button, cremini, shiitake, or portobello)

1/2 cup chopped yellow onion

1 clove garlic

2 sprigs thyme

1 tablespoon olive oil

1/2 cup water

Salt and freshly ground black pepper

PREHEAT the oven to 325°. Combine the mushrooms, onion, garlic, thyme, olive oil, and water in a small roasting pan, cover, and bake for 30 to 40 minutes, or until the mushrooms are tender. Remove from the oven, cool in the cooking juices, and season to taste with salt and pepper. Use immediately, or refrigerate for up to 3 days.

Preserved Ginger

YIELD: 1/4 CUP

6 tablespoons peeled and julienned fresh ginger

1 1/2 cups sugar

1 1/2 cups water

PLACE the ginger, 1/2 cup of the sugar, and 1/2 cup of the water in a small saucepan. Simmer for 10 minutes, strain the liquid, and repeat the process two more times, reserving the final cooking liquid to store the ginger. Use immediately, or refrigerate for up to 1 week.

Pickling Juice

YIELD: 2 CUPS

1 cup water

1/2 cup rice wine vinegar

1/3 cup plus 2 tablespoons sugar

2 tablespoons kosher salt

1 whole clove

1 teaspoon mustard seeds

1 teaspoon black peppercorns

1 teaspoon peeled and chopped fresh ginger

1/2 jalapeño, seeded and chopped

COMBINE all of the ingredients in a small saucepan and bring to a simmer over low heat, allowing the sugar and salt to dissolve. Cool and strain through a fine-mesh sieve. Use immediately, or refrigerate for up to 1 month.

Simple Syrup

YIELD: 1 1/2 CUPS

1 cup water

1 cup sugar

BRING the water and sugar to a boil in a small saucepan, remove from the heat, and cool. The syrup may be kept in the refrigerator for up to 1 month.

Curry Oil

1/2 cup chopped onion

1/2 cup chopped apple

2 cups plus 2 tablespoons grapeseed oil

Salt and pepper

1/4 cup curry powder

2 teaspoons turmeric

SAUTÉ the onion and apple in 2 tablespoons of grapeseed oil over medium heat, until just translucent. Season to taste with salt and pepper. Add the curry powder and turmeric and cook until the mixture starts to get pasty. Add the remaining grapeseed oil, mix well, and continue to cook until the oil is warm (do not boil). Thoroughly purée in a blender, pour into a container, and cover. Refrigerate for 2 days. Decant carefully.

Planning a Menu

Choosing a menu may seem like a simple task, but the combination of dishes can be the difference between a flawless meal and a huge headache. There are several things to consider when planning a multicourse menu. All dishes need to have contrasting and complementary flavors, colors, and textures. And, in a multicourse menu, each course needs to be considered within the context of the whole menu.

The progression of foods on a menu is a key to a successful meal. The menu should progress from delicately flavored to more strongly flavored dishes. Serving sautéed scallops after roasted garlic soup, for instance, may seem like a good idea, but after eating the garlic soup the delicate scallops will be tasteless. Start the menu with lighter dishes and move on to the heavier dishes. You should also serve cold dishes early in the progression and hot dishes later in the meal.

Contrasting textures are essential to an interesting menu. A dish with barley followed by a dish with Israeli couscous, for example, would be texturally repetitive—and boring— regardless of the variety in flavors.

Avoid using the same food twice in a single menu unless that food is the theme of your menu. Tomato soup followed by a course containing roasted tomatoes would be redundant in a regular menu. However, if you are planning a tomato menu, there should be tomatoes in every course.

Be cautious when using ethnic flavors in a meal. Combining more than two ethnic cuisines in one menu can be tricky, and most often it's just confusing.

Plan the wines to be served while planning the menu. Menus can progress from white to red wine, or they can be devoted only to red, or white, wine. (See below for a more detailed discussion on pairing food and wine.)

Consider cooking times and temperatures. Compare the cooking times, oven temperatures, and burner space of each recipe to make sure that the menu is feasible. If you have only one oven, you won't be able to cook two dishes that require different cooking temperatures and have them ready at the same time.

Pairing Food and Wine

For many people choosing the correct wine is the most intimidating part of planning a dinner party. Although it's not quite as simple as white wine with fish and red wine with meat, unless you are a wine connoisseur, it doesn't need to be unduly complicated. When pairing wine with food, the key is balance. Balancing the flavors involves considering the entire dish—its main components, the cooking technique, and the herbs or spices used.

First and foremost, the main characteristics of the wine should balance the main flavors of the dish. Oily foods, for example, should be served with crisp, acidic wines that cut through the oil. Salty foods are best with effervescent or high-alcohol wines to offset the salt. Smoked salmon served with caviar would call for a high-acid, effervescent wine. The effervescence tames the saltiness of the caviar, and the acid cuts through the fat in the salmon. Meaty-fat foods such as beef need wine with some tannin to cut through the fat.

When planning your wine selections, think about the prominent flavors in the dish. Is it grilled, cooked in butter, or broiled? Does it have an herb component that stands out? How does the sauce affect the flavor? Sautéed salmon with a mushroom–red wine sauce is best with an earthy, aromatic Pinot Noir. The wine will have enough acid to cut through the fat in the salmon, an earthiness to match the mushroom flavor, and a lightness that will allow the flavors of the dish to come through. But, if the salmon is served with a spicy Asian-flavored sauce, it would be best with a dry Gewürztraminer from Alsace, the rich brown-spice characteristics of which will highlight the Asian spices while handling the oiliness of the salmon.

Armed with a basic idea of the flavors in the menu, you can head to the local wine shop and peruse the selection. Don't be afraid to ask questions and to accept suggestions; the staff is there to help.

Once you have made your wine selections, make a note of them and keep them where they can be referenced later. The next time you prepare that dish, the notes can be used as a guide. Through trial and error, and note keeping, you will develop your food-and-wine-pairing knowledge.

Sample Menus

These menus can be followed exactly or used as a guideline for choosing your own combinations of dishes. The wine suggestions will give you a start on the direction for the wines.

MENU 1

This is a wonderful spring or summer menu, light and simple to prepare. It is one of those meals that is great shared among friends. The timing is not crucial, as much of the meal can be prepared in advance, and conversation can rule the evening.

Shrimp with Spicy Fruit Salsa (page 19)
Spätlese Riesling offers a sweetness to complement the fruit and foil the spice.

Olive Oil–Poached Cod with Roasted Tomatoes and Broccoli Rabe (page 85)
White Rhône, with its characteristic rich texture and
herbal flair, will handle the earthy vegetables.

Warm Peach Turnovers with Almond Ice Cream (page 194)
Sémillon-based wine, particularly Sauternes, will mirror the fruit and nut flavors.

PREPARATION TIPS

- For the starter, the tropical fruit can be cleaned, diced, and refrigerated in separate containers for several hours before serving. The vinaigrette can be prepared several hours in advance and tossed with the fruit just prior to serving.

- For the entrée, the tomatoes can be blanched, tossed with the other ingredients, and refrigerated until ready to bake. The broccoli rabe can be cleaned, blanched, and refrigerated for several hours.

- For the dessert, the ice cream can be prepared a day in advance. The dough can be rolled, cut, and refrigerated for several hours. The peaches and sauce can be prepared several hours in advance and refrigerated in separate containers.

MENU 2

This is a perfect fall or winter menu, full of warm, comforting foods. A nice glass of red wine is a must for sipping while preparing this meal.

Braised Leek Soup with Sautéed Oyster Mushrooms (page 50)
A Marsanne-based wine with rich texture and earthy
mineral tones ties in the mushrooms.

Rack of Lamb with Crispy Polenta and Mustard Sauce (page 142)
A complex Bordeaux with some age will show well against the lamb.

Cinnamon-Cranberry Bread Pudding with Vanilla Anglaise (page 206)
Gewürztraminer will have enough sweetness to contrast the bitter cranberries.

PREPARATION TIPS

- For the starter, the soup can be prepared several hours ahead and warmed just prior to serving. The mushrooms can be cleaned several hours ahead.

- For the entrée, the polenta can be prepared a day ahead and sautéed just prior to serving.

- The pudding can be prepared several hours ahead and refrigerated until ready to bake.

MENU 3

This is an ideal menu for a casual occasion. The tart can be served as guests arrive, the soup can be the first course at the table, and the dessert can wait for a break in conversation.

Bacon and Caramelized Onion Tart (page 33)
An aged Meursault with smoky mineral aromas will highlight the bacon, and its rich texture will emphasize the sweet onions.

Pumpkin Soup with Chicken and Ginger-Braised Leeks (page 46)
Alsatian Gewürztraminer will match the sweet flesh of the pumpkin and tie in the ginger.

Sautéed Veal Chops with Braised Juniper Berry–Infused Red Cabbage (page 135)
The ideal would be a Burgundy delicate enough not to overwhelm the veal but with enough acid to handle the cabbage.

Warm Apple-Date Tart with Honey-Caramel Sauce (page 180)
Choose a botrityzed dessert wine that encompasses the apple flavor while providing enough viscosity and sweetness to meet the caramel sauce.

PREPARATION TIPS

- For the starters, the tart shell can be prepared several hours ahead. The onions and bacon can be prepared ahead and refrigerated for several hours. Assemble the tart just prior to cooking.

- The soup and the leeks can be prepared several hours in advance and warmed separately just prior to serving.

- For the entrée, the red cabbage can be prepared several hours ahead and warmed just prior to serving.

- For the dessert, the tart can be assembled several hours in advance and baked just prior to serving.

MENU 4

Crab cakes make a great snack while you're grilling the tenderloin and making the salad. This is not a light menu—serve it at a leisurely pace, and make sure you invite hungry guests!

Crab Cakes with Sweet Curry–Red Bell Pepper Sauce (page 20)
Choose a Pinot Gris with richness to match the shellfish and enough residual sugar to contrast the spice of the bell pepper.

Grilled Beef Tenderloin and Blue Cheese Salad (page 57)
An Alsatian Gewürztraminer pairs well with the cheese and has enough richness for the meat.

Cumin-Garlic-Rubbed Cornish Hens with Potato-Parmesan Pavé (page 113)
Look for a low-alcohol Mosel Riesling Spätlese with delicate sweetness to contrast the spice of the cumin and the saltiness of the Parmesan.

Key Lime Pudding Cake with Dried-Fruit Compote (page 200)
A late-harvest Riesling with abundant fruit flavors and zesty, limey acidity will complement the cake.

PREPARATION TIPS

- For the starters, the crab cakes can be coated with the bread crumbs and refrigerated for several hours. Cook the cakes just prior to serving.

- The beef can be cooked, diced, and refrigerated for several hours. The vinaigrette can be prepared several hours ahead.

- For the entrée, the pavé can be prepared a day ahead and sautéed just prior to serving. The hens can be cleaned, rubbed with the spices, and refrigerated for several hours.

- For the dessert, the pudding cake can be prepared up to a day ahead.

MENU 5

*This menu has a strong Asian direction and could be served
with a great bottle of sake. Edamame (fresh soybeans) would
be a nice addition to the beginning of the meal.*

Shrimp Maki Rolls with Roasted Red Bell Pepper Aioli (page 22)
Choose a Crémant d'Alsace with the texture to stand up to the
rich shellfish and aromatics to highlight the Asian spices.

Egg Drop Soup with Ginger-Braised Chicken (page 44)
Blanc de Blancs Champagne has the texture to match the
soup and the effervescence to highlight the ginger.

Cilantro-Crusted Tuna Loin with Bok Choy and Lemon-Sesame Vinaigrette (page 78)
A New World sparkling wine with forward fruit and crisp
toastiness is an excellent complement to the meaty fish.

Chilled Peach Soup with Lemongrass Sorbet (page 172)
A sparkling dessert wine that is not too sweet will complement
the fruit and remain refreshing to match the sorbet.

PREPARATION TIPS

- For the starters, the roasted red bell pepper aioli can be prepared several hours ahead.

- The maki rolls should be assembled just prior to serving.

- The chicken can be braised a day ahead and warmed with a little bit of the soup just prior to serving. The soup can be prepared a day ahead. Warm the soup and stir in the egg just before serving.

- For the entrée, the lemon-sesame vinaigrette can be prepared several hours ahead. The bok choy can be cleaned and sliced several hours in advance.

- For the dessert, the soup and the sorbet can be prepared a day ahead.

MENU 6

This menu is a hit with diners who like the four basic food groups: vegetables, fish, meat, and chocolate. The menu starts off with nice, light, clean flavors and finishes with a rich chocolate dessert, giving a sense of complete balance.

Chilled Asparagus and Basil Soup with Goat Cheese (page 40)
Choose a Loire Valley Sauvignon Blanc with crispness
to complement the goat cheese and herbs.

Sautéed Sweet and Sour Cod with Oyster Mushrooms and Somen Noodles (page 83)
A New World Chardonnay with tropical overtones and good acid will
complement the cod and balance the sweet and sour flavors.

Grilled Strip Loin Steaks with Rosemary-Potato Purée and Meat Jus (page 129)
Fruity, spicy red Zinfandel with herbal tones is a great match for the rosemary.

Ginger-Chocolate Ganache Tart with Poached Pears (page 184)
A fortified Grenache from southwest France will combine
with the chocolate and accent the poached pears.

PREPARATION TIPS

- For the starters, the soup can be prepared a day ahead.

- The sweet and sour sauce for the cod can be prepared several days ahead. The oyster mushrooms can be cleaned and diced several hours ahead.

- For the entrée, the meat stock reduction can be prepared several days ahead. The steaks can marinate for up to 2 hours. The potatoes can be peeled and cut and kept in cold water until it is time to cook.

- For the dessert, the tart can be prepared up to a day ahead. The pears can be poached several hours ahead and warmed in the poaching liquid just prior to serving.

MENU 7

*Even though this appears to be a long menu, the food is
light and refreshing. The brochettes can be served alongside
the risotto to reduce the amount of plate washing.*

Goat Cheese-Stuffed Cherry Tomatoes (page 36)

Choose a New Zealand Sauvignon Blanc with acidity to match the
goat cheese and a tomato-herb flavor to match the tomatoes.

Sweet Corn and Shrimp Chowder (page 45)

A rich, opulent, oaky Chardonnay will complement the richness of the chowder.

Grilled Scallop and Red Onion Brochettes (page 95)

Choose a Meursault or Chardonnay with a little toasty flavor
to balance the rich scallops and sweet onions.

Spring Pea Risotto with Spicy Herb Sauce (page 164)

Sauvignon Blanc with good texture and little or no oak complements the herbal risotto.

Vanilla Crème Brûlée with Chocolate Sauce (page 211)

Madeira will complement both the chocolate and burnt sugar elements.

PREPARATION TIPS

- For the starters, the stuffed tomatoes can be prepared several hours ahead and refrigerated.

- The chowder can be prepared a day ahead and warmed just before serving.

- For the entrée, the marinade can be prepared a day ahead. The brochettes can be marinated for 2 hours, removed from the marinade, and refrigerated for several hours.

- The spicy herb sauce can be prepared several hours ahead. The risotto can be cooked three-quarters of the way and finished just before serving.

- For the dessert, the crème brûlée can be prepared several hours ahead and caramelized prior to serving.

MENU 8

This menu can be served family style for a casual meal or plated for a more elegant evening. The tapenade can be served before the meal or with the meal as the bread.

Kalamata Olive and Goat Cheese Tapenade (page 35)
Pinot Gris has enough residual sugar to counteract the bitterness of the olives.

Curry-Braised Chicken and Potato Tarts (page 28)
A Sémillon-based wine will have enough spice to stand up to
the curry and the waxy viscosity to support the potato.

Peppered Lamb Loin with Mustard Spaetzle and Thyme Reduction (page 145)
California Cabernet Sauvignon will complement the lamb and the thyme.

Warm Apple Cider Soup with Crispy Apple Turnovers (page 168)
Beerenauslese or Trockenbeerenauslese Rieslings will complement the
apples but contain enough acidity to keep the flavors of the soup fresh.

German Chocolate Cake with Toasted Pecan Sauce (page 197)
Tawny port will carry sweetness for the cake and mirror the nuttiness of the pecan.

PREPARATION TIPS

- For the starters, the bread can be prepared a day ahead and kept in an airtight container. The tapenade can be prepared several hours ahead and warmed to room temperature before serving.

- The chicken can be braised and the sauce prepared a day ahead and warmed just prior to serving. The tarts can be assembled several hours ahead and brushed with egg and baked just before serving.

- For the entrée, the meat stock reduction can be prepared several days ahead. The spaetzle can be prepared several hours ahead and warmed in a sauté pan with a little butter.

- For the dessert, the soup can be prepared a day ahead and warmed just prior to serving. The turnovers and the cake can be prepared several hours ahead.

STARTERS
appetizers | soups | salads

appetizers

19 | Shrimp with Spicy Fruit Salsa

20 | Crab Cakes with Sweet Curry–Red Bell Pepper Sauce

23 | Shrimp Maki Rolls with Roasted Red Bell Pepper Aioli

24 | Lobster and Sweet Corn Ravioli with Sweet Corn Broth

25 | Seared Tuna with Wasabi Sauce on Whole Wheat–Cumin Crackers

26 | Smoked Salmon Tartare with Horseradish Cream

28 | Curry-Braised Chicken and Potato Tarts

30 | Crispy Chicken Wontons with Apricot-Curry Sauce

31 | Grilled Tamari Beef with Shiitake Mushrooms and Daikon

33 | Bacon and Caramelized Onion Tart

34 | Spring Rolls with Sweet and Sour Yogurt Sauce

35 | Kalamata Olive and Goat Cheese Tapenade

36 | Goat Cheese–Stuffed Cherry Tomatoes

38 | Tiny Red Potatoes Stuffed with Caramelized Onions, Golden Raisins, and Walnuts

Shrimp with Spicy Fruit Salsa

SERVES 4

SALSA

$^1\!/_2$ cup diced mango

$^1\!/_2$ cup diced papaya

$^1\!/_2$ cup diced fresh pineapple

1 tablespoon freshly squeezed orange juice

1 tablespoon freshly squeezed lime juice

2 teaspoons chopped fresh cilantro

$^1\!/_4$ cup extra virgin olive oil

$^1\!/_4$ Thai chile, seeded and minced

8 large shrimp, peeled and deveined

Salt and freshly ground black pepper

1 tablespoon canola oil

TO PREPARE THE SALSA: Combine the mango, papaya, and pineapple in a medium bowl. Whisk together the orange juice, lime juice, cilantro, olive oil, and Thai chile in a small bowl and pour the mixture over the fruit. Toss lightly to coat the fruit.

TO PREPARE THE SHRIMP: Season the shrimp with salt and pepper and cook in a very hot sauté pan with the canola oil for 1 to 2 minutes on each side, or until just cooked.

Spoon some of the fruit salsa onto each plate and top with 2 shrimp.

> Thai chiles are small, dark green peppers with a lot of heat. They are available in many grocery stores, but if they aren't available in your area, use serrano or jalapeño chiles instead.

Crab Cakes with Sweet Curry–
Red Bell Pepper Sauce

SERVES 6

SAUCE

$1/2$ cup mayonnaise

$1/2$ roasted red bell pepper
(see page 5)

$1/2$ teaspoon minced garlic

$1/2$ teaspoon sweet curry powder

Salt and freshly ground
black pepper

CRAB CAKES

$3/4$ cup bread crumbs

$1^1/2$ tablespoons chopped
fresh parsley

12 ounces lump crabmeat, cleaned

3 tablespoons diced red
bell pepper

1 jalapeño chile, seeded
and chopped

2 tablespoons chopped
fresh chives

2 teaspoons freshly squeezed
lime juice

Salt and freshly ground
black pepper

2 tablespoons canola oil

6 teaspoons curry oil (see page 6)

1 tablespoon baby mizuna

TO MAKE THE SAUCE: Purée the mayonnaise, bell pepper, garlic, and curry powder until smooth. Season to taste with salt and pepper.

TO PREPARE THE CRAB CAKES: Combine the bread crumbs and parsley in a small bowl and set aside. Place the crabmeat in a medium bowl. Fold in the bell pepper, jalapeño, chives, and lime juice and season to taste with salt and pepper. Fold in $1/4$ cup of the bread crumb mixture and 5 tablespoons of the sauce.

Divide the crab mixture into 18 equal portions and form into small patties. Cut each patty into a $1^1/2$-inch square. Dredge the crab cakes in the remaining bread crumbs. Cook the crab cakes in the canola oil in a hot sauté pan for 2 to 3 minutes on each side, or until golden brown and crispy.

Place three crab cakes on each plate and drizzle a small spoonful of the sauce around the cakes. Lightly drizzle 1 teaspoon of the curry oil onto the plate. Garnish with baby mizuna. Serve warm.

> It is easy to make bread crumbs at home. Allow any type of bread to dry out completely, grind it in a food processor or blender until fine, and pass the crumbs through a sieve to remove any large pieces. If you don't have time to let the bread dry naturally, place it in a 200° oven for 15 to 20 minutes, or until dry. You may also use a toaster to dry the bread. You can experiment with different types of bread, but sourdough bread adds a particularly tantalizing flavor.
> You'll need to make the curry oil 2 days in advance.

Shrimp Maki Rolls with Roasted Red Bell Pepper Aioli

SERVES 4

AIOLI

¼ cup chopped roasted red bell pepper (see page 5)

¼ cup mayonnaise

2 teaspoons freshly squeezed lemon juice

Salt and freshly ground black pepper

FILLING

⅓ cup sushi (or maki) rice

1 cup water

1½ tablespoons sugar

2 tablespoons rice wine vinegar

4 ounces cooked shrimp, chopped

2 scallions, chopped

Salt and freshly ground black pepper

2 sheets nori

1 teaspoon long cut fresh chives

2 teaspoons scallion (white part only), thinly sliced

> Although it may be tempting to prepare the maki rolls ahead of time and refrigerate them, don't do it. Refrigerating completely changes their texture.

TO PREPARE THE AIOLI: Purée the bell pepper, mayonnaise, and lemon juice until smooth. Season to taste with salt and pepper.

TO PREPARE THE FILLING: Rinse the rice under cold running water until the water runs clear. Combine the rice and water in a small saucepan and simmer over medium-low heat for 20 to 25 minutes, or until tender. Cool to room temperature. Combine the sugar and vinegar in a small bowl, pour over the rice, and stir gently until mixed.

Combine the shrimp and scallions in a medium bowl and season to taste with salt and pepper.

TO PREPARE THE MAKI ROLL: Lay a sheet of nori on a maki roller or a piece of plastic wrap. Place ½ cup of the rice on top of the nori. With moist hands, spread the rice flat, leaving a 2-inch border at the top of the nori. Spread 1 tablespoon of the aioli over the rice. Spoon half of the shrimp mixture across the middle of the rice.

Using the maki roller or the plastic wrap, start from the bottom and carefully roll up the nori sheet, creating a firm, smooth maki roll. Moisten the 2-inch border of the nori with water and fold over the roll to create a seal. Set aside and repeat the process with the remaining ingredients.

Let the maki rolls stand for 5 minutes at room temperature, and then slice them into 1½-inch pieces. Place six pieces of maki on each dish and lightly spoon some of the aioli along the side of the roll. Garnish with chives and scallion. Serve with the remaining aioli as a dipping sauce.

Lobster and Sweet Corn Ravioli with Sweet Corn Broth

SERVES 4

BROTH

10 ears sweet corn

2 bay leaves

Salt and freshly ground black pepper

RAVIOLI

2 tablespoons unsalted butter

1 yellow onion, finely diced

6 ounces cooked lobster tail meat, diced

Salt and freshly ground black pepper

12 3-inch square wonton skins (see note, page 157)

1 egg, lightly beaten

3 fresh basil leaves, cut into thin strands

TO PREPARE THE BROTH: Remove the kernels from the cobs, reserving the kernels and cobs. Place the cobs, bay leaves, and half of the kernels in a stockpot, cover with water, and simmer over low heat for 1 hour. Strain through a fine-mesh sieve. Place the broth in a saucepan and cook over medium heat for 10 to 20 minutes, or until reduced to 3 cups. Season to taste with salt and pepper. Keep warm.

TO PREPARE THE RAVIOLI FILLING: Melt the butter in a sauté pan over medium heat. Add the onion and cook for 5 minutes, or until translucent. Add the remaining corn kernels and cook for 10 to 12 minutes, or until tender. Purée the corn mixture until smooth, add the lobster, and season to taste with salt and pepper.

TO PREPARE THE RAVIOLI: Bring a large pot of salted water to a boil. Place 1 tablespoon of filling in the center of each wonton skin and brush 2 adjoining edges with the egg. Fold the wonton skins in half to form triangles and press firmly to seal the edges. (The ravioli can be prepared to this point several hours ahead of time and refrigerated on a lightly floured sheet pan.) Cook the ravioli in the boiling water for 3 to 4 minutes, or until al dente, then drain.

Arrange 3 ravioli in the bottom of each bowl and ladle in the broth. Top with pepper and sprinkle with the basil.

> The French term for thinly sliced strands of greens is *chiffonade* (shee-foh-nahd), a cut generally used for leafy vegetables or herbs. To chiffonade the basil for this recipe, stack the leaves on top of one another and roll them up. Cut into 1/16-inch-wide strips across the roll.

Seared Tuna with Wasabi Sauce
on Whole Wheat–Cumin Crackers

SERVES 8

CRACKERS

1 tablespoon all-purpose flour

$1/2$ cup whole wheat flour

$1/2$ teaspoon baking powder

$1/4$ teaspoon cumin seeds, coarsely ground

$1/8$ teaspoon salt

1 tablespoon wheat germ

1 tablespoon cold unsalted butter, plus 2 tablespoons melted

$1/4$ cup milk

1 tablespoon kosher salt

2 tablespoons sesame seeds

SAUCE

1 teaspoon wasabi powder

2 teaspoons mirin (see note, page 31)

$1/2$ cup mayonnaise

TUNA

4 ounces sashimi-grade tuna loin

2 tablespoons canola oil

Salt and freshly ground black pepper

TO PREPARE THE CRACKERS: Preheat the oven to 450°. Sift together the all-purpose flour, whole wheat flour, baking powder, cumin, salt, and wheat germ and place in a food processor. Add the cold butter and pulse until a coarse meal forms. Add the milk and pulse for 20 seconds. Remove and form into a ball.

On a floured surface, roll out the dough $1/16$ inch thick and cut out 32 $1^1/_2$-inch-diameter circles. Prick each circle several times with a fork and place on a buttered baking sheet. Brush the crackers with the melted butter and sprinkle with the salt and sesame seeds. Bake for 8 to 10 minutes, or until lightly browned. Cool and store in an airtight container until ready to use.

TO PREPARE THE SAUCE: Mix the wasabi with the mirin in a small bowl. Mix in the mayonnaise. Refrigerate until needed.

TO PREPARE THE TUNA: Cut the tuna lengthwise into quarters. Rub with the canola oil and season with salt and pepper. Cook in a sauté pan over medium-high heat for 15 to 20 seconds on each side, or until just browned. Cut each piece into $1/8$-inch-thick slices.

Overlap 2 tuna slices on each cracker and top with a dab of sauce.

> Sashimi-grade is the freshest, highest-quality tuna available. Because the tuna in this recipe is left raw in the middle, it is extremely important to buy only the highest-quality tuna from a reputable fish market. Wasabi is the Japanese version of horseradish. It has a sharp, pungent, fiery flavor and can be found in paste and powder form.

Smoked Salmon Tartare with Horseradish Cream

SERVES 4

3 tablespoons olive oil

12 thin 2-inch-diameter circles sourdough bread

¼ cup heavy cream

1 tablespoon plus 1 teaspoon finely grated fresh horseradish

2 teaspoons finely chopped fresh chives

Salt and freshly ground black pepper

¾ cup finely diced smoked salmon

3 tablespoons chopped fresh chervil

1½ tablespoons chopped capers

1½ tablespoons chopped shallots

1 teaspoon fresh fennel bulb top (thin green part only)

TO PREPARE THE BREAD: Preheat the oven to 350°. Using 2 tablespoons of the olive oil, brush each side of the bread circles with oil and place on a baking sheet. Toast in the oven for 10 minutes, or until golden brown. Remove from the oven and set aside.

TO PREPARE THE CREAM: Place the cream in a small bowl and whip with a whisk for 2 minutes, or until soft peaks just begin to form. Stir in the 1 tablespoon horseradish and the chives and season to taste with salt and pepper.

TO PREPARE THE SALMON: Place the salmon, chervil, capers, shallots, and the remaining 1 tablespoon olive oil in a small bowl and mix thoroughly. Season to taste with pepper.

Place 3 pieces of the toasted sourdough in the center of each plate and top with a small spoonful of the horseradish cream. Spoon some of the smoked salmon tartare over the cream, top with freshly ground black pepper, and garnish with the fennel tops and the 1 teaspoon grated horseradish. Serve immediately.

> If you prefer to pass these appetizers rather than serve them on a plate, use 24 circles of bread only 1 inch in diameter and proceed as directed.

Curry-Braised Chicken and Potato Tarts

SERVES 6

DOUGH

1 1/2 cups flour

1 teaspoon salt

1 cup cold unsalted butter, chopped

1/3 cup ice water

FILLING

4 chicken thighs, boned

Salt and freshly ground black pepper

1 tablespoon canola oil

1 yellow onion, chopped

1 carrot, peeled and chopped

1 stalk celery, chopped

1 tablespoon curry powder

2 cups chicken stock (see page 4)

1 large potato, peeled and cut into 1/8-inch-thick disks

1 egg yolk, lightly beaten

TO PREPARE THE DOUGH: Place the flour, salt, and butter in a medium bowl. Using a pastry cutter or fork, cut the butter into the flour until it forms pea-sized chunks. Add the water and mix with a fork until the dough just comes together (it should have visible streaks of butter). Form the dough into a disk, wrap in plastic wrap, and refrigerate for at least 1 hour.

TO BRAISE THE CHICKEN: Season the chicken with salt and pepper. Heat the canola oil in a large sauté pan over medium heat, add the chicken, and cook for 2 minutes on each side, or until golden brown. Add the onion, carrot, and celery to the pan and cook for 8 to 10 minutes, or until the vegetables are caramelized. Add the curry powder and cook for 2 minutes. Add the stock, cover, and cook over medium-low heat for 50 to 60 minutes, or until the chicken is tender. Remove the chicken from the liquid and remove and discard the skin. Strain the braising liquid through a fine-mesh sieve and set aside. Shred the chicken and season to taste with salt and pepper.

TO PREPARE THE TARTS: On a floured surface, roll out the dough 1/8 inch thick. Cut 12 circles large enough to line and cover a 3-inch-diameter by 1/2-inch-high tartlet ring. Place 6 tartlet rings on a parchment-lined baking sheet and press a dough circle into each one. Press a 1/4-inch-thick layer of chicken in the bottom of each tartlet ring. Arrange the potato slices over the chicken to form 2 complete layers. Gently press the remaining chicken into the tartlet rings and cover with the remaining dough. Seal the edges, trimming any excess, and refrigerate the tarts for at least 30 minutes.

Preheat the oven to 375°. Brush the tops of the tarts with the egg and bake for 35 to 40 minutes, or until golden brown.

MEANWHILE, PREPARE THE SAUCE: Cook the reserved braising liquid over medium-high heat for 20 to 30 minutes, or until reduced to about $3/4$ cup. Season to taste with salt and pepper and set aside.

Remove the tarts from the oven, let stand for 5 minutes, and cut in half. Place 2 halves in a **V** shape in the center of each plate. Spoon the warm sauce around the tarts.

Serving individual tarts to each guest is a great presentation, but if you don't have small tart rings, this recipe can also be made as an 8- or 9-inch tart. Simply cut the dough to fit your pan and follow the directions for layering the ingredients. The cooking time for a larger tart may be slightly longer.

Crispy Chicken Wontons
with Apricot-Curry Sauce

SERVES 6

SAUCE

1/2 cup dried apricots

2/3 cup water

1/4 cup rice wine vinegar

1 teaspoon hot curry powder

WONTONS

1 boneless, skinless chicken breast

Salt and freshly ground
black pepper

2 teaspoons canola oil

1/4 cup raisins, chopped

1/2 cup chopped scallions

24 small round wonton skins
(see note, page 157)

1 egg, lightly beaten

3 tablespoons unsalted butter

TO PREPARE THE SAUCE: Purée the apricots, water, vinegar, and curry powder until smooth. Strain through a fine-mesh sieve and store in the refrigerator. Warm just prior to serving.

TO PREPARE THE FILLING: Season the chicken breast with salt and pepper. Heat the canola oil in a sauté pan over medium heat, add the chicken, and cook for 5 to 6 minutes on each side, or until just cooked. Finely dice the chicken breast and place in a small bowl. Stir in the raisins and scallions and season to taste with salt and pepper.

TO PREPARE THE WONTONS: Spoon some of the chicken mixture into the center of each wonton. Lightly brush the edges of each wonton with the egg, fold in half to form a half-moon, and press firmly on the edges to seal. (The wontons can be prepared several hours ahead and refrigerated on a floured sheet pan.)

Bring a large pot of salted water to a boil. Cook the wontons for 3 to 4 minutes, or until al dente, then drain. Heat the butter in a large sauté pan over medium heat, add the wontons, and cook for 2 to 3 minutes on each side, or until golden brown.

Serve immediately with the warm apricot sauce for dipping.

Curry powder is actually a blend of several spices, typically turmeric, cinnamon, cardamom, cloves, nutmeg, and mace. It can also contain ground dried chiles, black pepper, and sesame seeds. Depending on the ratios of the spices, it can be made sweet or hot. Many stores carry both types, but if you can only find curry powder with no sweet or hot distinction, it probably sits in the middle or leans toward the sweeter side. If that is the case, a couple of dashes of cayenne pepper can be added to provide the heat. You can purchase apricot-curry sauce online at www.charlietrotters.com.

Grilled Tamari Beef with Shiitake Mushrooms and Daikon

SERVES 4

MARINADE

¹/₂ cup tamari

¹/₄ cup mirin

2 tablespoons peeled and minced fresh ginger

1¹/₂ tablespoons sesame oil

³/₄ pound sirloin steak

Salt and freshly ground black pepper

2 cups thinly sliced shiitake mushrooms

2 tablespoons canola oil

¹/₄ cup peeled and thinly sliced daikon

TO PREPARE THE MARINADE: Combine the tamari, mirin, ginger, and sesame oil in a small bowl.

TO PREPARE THE BEEF: Cut the sirloin into 12 strips, each 4 by 1 by ¹/₄ inch. Weave each strip onto a wooden skewer and season with salt and pepper. Reserve 2 tablespoons of the marinade in a small bowl. Brush the remaining marinade on the skewers. Place the skewers in a large resealable plastic bag and refrigerate for 2 hours.

Prepare a medium-hot grill.

Meanwhile, sauté the mushrooms in the canola oil over medium heat for 3 to 5 minutes, or until slightly soft. Add the daikon and cook for 2 minutes. Add the reserved marinade to the pan, toss quickly, and remove from the heat. Season to taste with salt and pepper.

Grill the skewers for 2 minutes on each side, or until cooked to the desired doneness.

Form a bed of the mushroom mixture in the center of each plate and top with 3 skewers. Top with freshly ground black pepper.

> Tamari, mirin, and daikon are all common Japanese ingredients. Tamari is similar to soy sauce but is thicker and has a more mellow flavor. Mirin is a low-alcohol, sweet, golden cooking wine made from rice. It is sometimes called rice wine, but don't confuse it with rice wine vinegar. Both items can be found in the Asian section of most grocery stores or in an Asian market. Daikon is a large Asian radish that looks like a big, smooth, white carrot. It has a flavor similar to that of a radish but slightly hotter. Daikon is available in most grocery stores.

Bacon and Caramelized Onion Tart

SERVES 6

DOUGH

2 cups flour

$1/2$ teaspoon salt

1 cup cold unsalted butter, chopped

$2/3$ cup ice water

FILLING

3 large yellow onions, julienned

2 tablespoons unsalted butter

Salt and freshly ground black pepper

1 pound bacon, julienned

1 egg yolk

$1/2$ cup heavy cream

2 teaspoons fresh thyme leaves

TO PREPARE THE DOUGH: Place the flour, salt, and butter in a medium bowl. Using a pastry cutter or fork, cut the butter into the flour until it forms pea-sized chunks. Add the water and mix with a fork until the dough just comes together (it should have visible streaks of butter). Form the dough into a disk, wrap in plastic wrap, and refrigerate for at least 1 hour.

TO PREPARE THE FILLING: Cook the onions with the butter in a large sauté pan over medium heat, stirring occasionally, for 15 to 20 minutes, or until the onions are golden brown and caramelized. Season with salt and pepper to taste and cool to room temperature.

Cook the bacon in a large sauté pan over medium heat for 10 minutes, or until crisp. Drain on paper towels and cool to room temperature. Combine the bacon with the onions.

Preheat the oven to 375°. Whisk together the egg yolk, cream, and thyme in a small bowl.

TO PREPARE THE TART: On a floured surface, roll out the dough $1/8$ inch thick, and then press into a baking dish that is about $1 1/4$-inches deep and about 8 or 9 inches in diameter. Crimp the edges of the dough along the top of the dish. Spoon the onion-bacon mixture on top of the dough, pour in the cream mixture, and top with freshly ground pepper.

Bake for 40 to 45 minutes, or until just firm to the touch and a light golden brown. Cool slightly before cutting and serving.

This tart can also be cut into 1-inch squares for canapés. To prepare the canapés ahead, cook according to the directions and cool completely. Just prior to serving, cut the tart into 1-inch squares, place the squares on a baking sheet, and place in a 350° oven for 10 minutes, or until warm.

Spring Rolls with
Sweet and Sour Yogurt Sauce

SERVES 4

SAUCE

1/4 cup plain yogurt

2 teaspoons sesame oil

2 tablespoons soy sauce

1 tablespoon Dijon mustard

1 tablespoon freshly
squeezed orange juice

1 tablespoon minced
preserved ginger

FILLING

3/4 cup finely julienned carrots

3/4 cup finely julienned leeks
(white part only)

3/4 cup finely julienned
red bell pepper

3/4 cup shredded napa cabbage

1 tablespoon freshly squeezed
lime juice

3 tablespoons fresh cilantro,
cut in thin strands

1/4 cup sesame oil

Salt and freshly ground
black pepper

4 8-inch round pieces rice paper

TO PREPARE THE SAUCE: Mix the yogurt, sesame oil, soy sauce, mustard, and orange juice in a small bowl until smooth. Stir in the ginger and set aside.

TO PREPARE THE FILLING: Toss together the carrots, leeks, bell pepper, cabbage, lime juice, and cilantro in a large bowl. Drizzle the sesame oil over the vegetables and season with salt and pepper to taste.

TO PREPARE THE SPRING ROLLS: Soak 1 piece of the rice paper in a bowl of cold water for 1 minute, or until slightly soft. Immediately remove the rice paper from the water or it will break apart. Lay the rice paper flat and place a quarter of the vegetable mixture toward the bottom of the paper. Roll up tightly, folding in the sides of the rice paper, until you have a tight, cigar-like shape. Repeat this process 3 more times with the remaining ingredients.

Slice each spring roll in half on the diagonal and serve with the sauce for dipping.

> Rice paper, a popular Vietnamese ingredient, is a thin, edible paper made from rice and traditionally dried in the sun. It must be soaked in cold water to soften before using and can be difficult to work with at first. The trick is to remove it from the water as soon as it's soft or it will tear (and to buy extra in case you don't act quickly enough). Rice paper can be found in the Asian section of grocery stores or in Asian markets.

Kalamata Olive and Goat Cheese Tapenade

SERVES 4

1 cup pitted kalamata olives, well drained and finely chopped

$1/2$ cup soft goat cheese

2 tablespoons chopped fresh chives

12 slices French bread

2 tablespoons extra virgin olive oil

TO PREPARE THE TAPENADE: Mix together the olives, goat cheese, and chives in a small bowl.

TO PREPARE THE BREAD: Preheat the oven to 350°. Brush both sides of the French bread slices with the olive oil and toast in the oven for 6 to 8 minutes, or until a light golden brown.

Spread some of the tapenade on each slice of bread and serve at room temperature.

Goat cheese comes in a wide variety of textures, ranging from soft and creamy to as hard as Parmesan. Soft goat cheese is readily available at most grocery stores; the firmer types usually require a trip to a specialty cheese shop.

Goat Cheese–Stuffed Cherry Tomatoes

SERVES 4

12 cherry tomatoes

FILLING

2 ounces soft goat cheese
(see note, page 35)

1 tablespoon chopped oil-
packed sundried tomatoes

1 tablespoon pine nuts, toasted
and coarsely chopped

$1/2$ teaspoon chopped fresh chives

$1/2$ teaspoon chopped fresh
flat-leaf parsley

Salt and freshly ground
black pepper

1 teaspoon fresh flat-leaf
parsley, stems removed

1 teaspoon grains of paradise

1 teaspoon pine nuts, toasted
and coarsely chopped

TO PREPARE THE TOMATOES: Cut a small **X** in the bottom of each tomato. Blanch the tomatoes in boiling water for 15 seconds and remove immediately. Peel, then cut $1/4$ inch off the top of each tomato. Using a melon baller, hollow out the tomatoes.

TO PREPARE THE FILLING: Combine the goat cheese, sun-dried tomatoes, pine nuts, chives, and parsley in a small bowl. Season to taste with salt and pepper.

Spoon some of the goat cheese mixture into each of the tomatoes and place in the refrigerator. Remove from the refrigerator 15 minutes before serving. Garnish with flat-leaf parsley, grains of paradise, and the pine nuts.

> Nuts should always be toasted before using them. Raw, they are bland and a little gummy; toasted, they have a wonderful, nutty flavor and a crunchy texture. To toast any type of nut, place them on a baking sheet in a preheated 350° oven for 10 minutes, or until a light golden brown and aromatic.

Tiny Red Potatoes Stuffed with Caramelized Onions, Golden Raisins, and Walnuts

SERVES 4

12 small red potatoes
(1 to 1$\frac{1}{2}$ inches in diameter)

1 tablespoon sour cream

Salt and freshly ground
black pepper

1$\frac{1}{2}$ cups julienned yellow onions

2 tablespoons extra virgin olive oil

$\frac{1}{4}$ cup golden raisins,
coarsely chopped

$\frac{1}{4}$ cup walnuts, toasted (see note,
page 36) and coarsely chopped

TO PREPARE THE POTATOES: Place the potatoes in a large pot of salted water, bring to a boil, and cook for 20 to 25 minutes, or until tender. Drain and refrigerate until chilled. Cut the tops off the potatoes and hollow out each potato with a melon baller, leaving sturdy walls and reserving the potato and the pulp.

TO PREPARE THE FILLING: Finely dice the potato pulp, fold in the sour cream, and season to taste with salt and pepper.

Cook the onions with the olive oil in a medium sauté pan over medium heat, stirring occasionally, for 15 to 20 minutes, or until caramelized. Add the raisins and walnuts and cook for 2 minutes. Season to taste with salt and pepper.

Fill the potato shells halfway with the potato mixture and top with some of the onion mixture. Refrigerate until ready to serve.

> These stuffed potatoes also make a great warm appetizer. Place in a preheated 350° oven for 10 minutes, or until warm. If you can't find very small red potatoes, buy the smallest ones you can find and cut them in half after cooking.

soups

40 | Chilled Asparagus and Basil Soup with Goat Cheese

41 | Chilled Fresh Tomato Soup

43 | Chilled Cucumber Soup with Kimchi

44 | Egg Drop Soup with Ginger-Braised Chicken

45 | Sweet Corn and Shrimp Chowder

46 | Pumpkin Soup with Chicken and Ginger-Braised Leeks

48 | Yellow Squash and Granny Smith Apple Soup with Preserved Squash

49 | Mushroom-Barley Soup

50 | Braised Leek Soup with Sautéed Oyster Mushrooms

51 | Vidalia Onion Soup with Wild Rice and Maytag Blue Cheese Croutons

52 | Roasted Garlic Soup with Chicken Liver Croutons

53 | Lentil and Bacon Soup

Chilled Asparagus and Basil Soup with Goat Cheese

SERVES 4

16 asparagus spears, trimmed and blanched

4 tablespoons extra virgin olive oil

3 cups vegetable stock (see page 4)

3 tablespoons chopped fresh basil

1 teaspoon minced garlic

Salt and freshly ground black pepper

4 ounces soft goat cheese (see note, page 35), crumbled into small pieces

3 fresh basil leaves, cut into thin strands (see note, page 24)

TO PREPARE THE ASPARAGUS SOUP: Cut the tips off the asparagus and set aside. Purée the asparagus stems, 3 tablespoons of the olive oil, the stock, basil, and garlic until smooth. Strain through a fine-mesh sieve and season to taste with salt and pepper. Refrigerate until thoroughly chilled.

Toss the asparagus tips with the remaining 1 tablespoon olive oil and season to taste with salt and pepper.

Ladle the soup into 4 shallow bowls and arrange 4 asparagus tips in the center of each bowl. Sprinkle the goat cheese and basil around the bowls and top with freshly ground pepper.

This soup would also be good with the addition of an acid or a sharp element such as peeled, seeded, and diced tomatoes or chopped Greek olives.

Chilled Fresh Tomato Soup

SERVES 4

TOMATO WATER

12 large beefsteak tomatoes

1 tablespoon salt

Freshly ground black pepper

SOUP

24 small red or yellow teardrop
tomatoes (see note, page 103),
halved

1/4 cup peeled and finely diced plum

1/4 cup finely diced zucchini

1/4 cup peeled and finely
diced apple

1/4 cup peeled and finely diced
cucumber

1 jalapeño chile, seeded
and finely minced

1 teaspoon finely chopped
fresh chives

1 teaspoon finely chopped
fresh basil

Freshly ground black pepper

4 teaspoons extra virgin olive oil

TO PREPARE THE TOMATO WATER: Purée the tomatoes and add the salt. Pour the purée into a cheesecloth-lined sieve set in a large bowl and refrigerate for 8 hours, or until all the juices have dripped from the purée. Discard the solids and season the tomato water to taste with salt and pepper. Refrigerate until ready to serve.

TO PREPARE THE SOUP: Arrange the cherry tomatoes, plum, zucchini, apple, cucumber, and jalapeño in the center of each shallow bowl. Ladle the tomato water into the bowls and sprinkle with the chives and basil. Top with freshly ground black pepper and drizzle with the olive oil.

> Tomato water gives this dish all of the flavor without the heaviness of the whole tomato. It is also good for adding flavor to risotto and other grains.

Chilled Cucumber Soup with Kimchi

SERVES 4

2 English cucumbers, peeled and chopped

1 cup plain yogurt

3 tablespoons freshly squeezed lemon juice

Salt and freshly ground black pepper

1 cup kimchi, drained

4 teaspoons amaranth, snow pea sprouts, or fresh chervil leaves

1 teaspoon olive oil

1/2 English cucumber, peeled and cut into thin sticks 1 inch long

TO PREPARE THE SOUP: Purée the two cucumbers, yogurt, and lemon juice until smooth and season to taste with salt and pepper. Refrigerate until thoroughly chilled.

Spoon some of the kimchi in the center of each bowl, ladle in the soup, and sprinkle with the amaranth. Add a dollop of yogurt on the side, if desired. Garnish with a drizzle of olive oil and extra cucumber cut into sticks.

Kimchi is a spicy, pungent, pickled, fermented cabbage that is served at almost every Korean meal. It is usually found in jars in the produce section of the grocery store. Making kimchi from scratch takes at least 3 days. If you can't find it at the store, just substitute the following: Cut 4 leaves of napa cabbage into large, bite-sized pieces. Heat 1 teaspoon sesame oil in a large sauté pan over medium heat, add 2 teaspoons peeled and minced fresh ginger and 2 teaspoons rice vinegar, and cook for 1 minute. Add the napa cabbage and cook, stirring frequently, for 3 minutes, or until the leaves are wilted and the stems are still slightly crunchy. Refrigerate until chilled.

If English cucumbers are not available, use regular cucumbers and scrape out the seeds.

Egg Drop Soup with Ginger-Braised Chicken

SERVES 4

4 chicken thighs, boned

Salt and freshly ground
black pepper

1 tablespoon canola oil

1 yellow onion, chopped

1 carrot, peeled and chopped

1 stalk celery, chopped

1/4 cup peeled and chopped
fresh ginger

2 quarts chicken stock (see page 4)

1/2 cup lemon thyme sprigs

1 egg, lightly beaten

2 tablespoons chopped scallions

TO BRAISE THE CHICKEN: Season the chicken with salt and pepper. Heat the canola oil in a large sauté pan over medium-high heat, add the chicken, and cook for 2 minutes on each side, or until golden brown. Add the onion, carrot, and celery to the pan and cook, stirring occasionally, for 8 to 10 minutes, or until the vegetables are caramelized. Add the ginger and cook for 2 minutes. Add the chicken stock to the pan, cover, and cook over medium-low heat for 30 to 40 minutes, or until the chicken is tender. Remove the chicken from the liquid and remove and discard the skin. Strain the braising liquid through a fine-mesh sieve, skim and discard the fat, and set aside. Cut the chicken into bite-sized pieces.

TO PREPARE THE SOUP: Place the reserved braising liquid in a medium saucepan and bring to a simmer over medium heat. Add the lemon thyme and simmer for 3 minutes. Strain through a fine-mesh sieve and season to taste with salt and pepper. Return the liquid to the saucepan and bring it to a gentle simmer over medium-low heat. Slowly stir in the egg and immediately remove the pan from the heat.

Place some of the chicken in the center of each bowl. Ladle the soup into the bowls, sprinkle with the scallions, and top with freshly ground black pepper.

Lemon thyme can sometimes be difficult for a home cook to find. If you aren't able to purchase it, use regular thyme and a scant 1/2 teaspoon finely grated lemon zest.

Sweet Corn and Shrimp Chowder

SERVES 6

10 ears sweet corn

2 bay leaves

4 quarts water

Salt and freshly ground
black pepper

1 cup heavy cream

8 ounces bacon, julienned

1 small yellow onion, chopped

1 large potato, peeled and diced

12 ounces shrimp, peeled, deveined,
and cut into bite-sized pieces

2 tablespoons chopped
fresh chives

TO PREPARE THE BROTH: Remove the kernels from the cobs, reserving the kernels. Place the cobs, bay leaves, and water in a stockpot and simmer over medium-low heat for 1 hour. Strain through a fine-mesh sieve and discard the solids. Season to taste with salt and pepper.

TO PREPARE THE CHOWDER: Place half of the corn kernels in a small saucepan with the cream and cook over medium heat for 8 to 10 minutes, or until the cream is reduced to about $2/3$ cup. Purée the mixture until smooth.

Cook the bacon in a large sauté pan over medium-low heat for 5 minutes, or until the fat is translucent. Add the onion, potato, and the remaining corn and cook for 10 to 12 minutes, or until the potatoes are tender. Add the shrimp and cook, stirring continuously, for 2 to 3 minutes, or until the shrimp are just cooked. Season to taste with salt and pepper.

Place the corn purée in a large saucepan over medium-low heat and add the corn broth 1 cup at a time until the desired consistency is reached. Add the sautéed corn mixture and cook for 5 minutes, or until warm. Season to taste with salt and pepper.

Ladle the soup into bowls, sprinkle with the chives, and top with freshly ground black pepper.

> This chowder is also great with lobster in place of the shrimp, or as corn chowder, with no seafood at all. Any extra corn broth can be frozen for several months.

Pumpkin Soup with Chicken and Ginger-Braised Leeks

SERVES 4

1 small pumpkin, halved and seeded

Salt and freshly ground black pepper

3 tablespoons extra virgin olive oil, plus extra for drizzling

8 sprigs thyme

2 leeks (white part only), cut into 1/4-inch-thick slices

5 tablespoons unsalted butter

3 cups chicken stock (see page 4)

1 tablespoon plus 1/4 cup preserved ginger (see page 6)

2 boneless, skinless chicken breasts

1 tablespoon canola oil

2 teaspoons fresh tiny sage leaves

This is a perfect dish for entertaining, as the soup and leeks can be prepared several hours ahead.

TO PREPARE THE PUMPKIN: Preheat the oven to 350°. Season the flesh of the pumpkin with salt and pepper and rub with the olive oil. Place the pumpkin halves, cut side down, on a baking sheet and place 4 thyme sprigs under each half. Add 1/4 inch water to the pan and roast for 45 to 60 minutes, or until tender. Scrape the pulp into a bowl and discard the skin.

MEANWHILE, PREPARE THE LEEKS: Cook the leeks with 2 tablespoons of the butter in a saucepan over medium heat for 10 minutes, or until translucent. Add 1 cup of the stock and the 1 tablespoon ginger and cook over medium-low heat for 25 minutes, or until the leeks are soft and most of the liquid has been absorbed. Keep warm.

TO PREPARE THE CHICKEN: Season the chicken breasts with salt and pepper. Heat the canola oil in a sauté pan over medium heat, add the chicken breasts, and cook for 5 to 6 minutes on each side, or until just cooked. Thinly slice the chicken and reserve.

TO PREPARE THE SOUP: Purée the 1/4 cup ginger and any residual ginger juice, the remaining 2 cups stock, and the pumpkin pulp until smooth. Season with salt and pepper. Cook the soup in a saucepan over medium heat for 5 minutes, or until warm. Whisk in the remaining 3 tablespoons butter and season with salt and pepper.

Spoon some of the leeks into the center of each bowl and ladle the soup around the leeks. Arrange some of the sliced chicken in the center of each bowl and sprinkle with tiny sage leaves. Drizzle with olive oil and serve immediately.

Yellow Squash and Granny Smith
Apple Soup with Preserved Squash

SERVES 4

1/2 cup finely diced yellow squash

1 cup pickling juice (see page 6)

1 cup chopped yellow onions

1 tablespoon extra virgin olive oil

3 cups peeled and chopped
yellow squash

2 cups peeled and chopped
Granny Smith apples

2 cups water

1 teaspoon ground turmeric

Salt and freshly ground
black pepper

1 tablespoon chopped fresh chervil

TO PREPARE THE PRESERVED SQUASH: Put the diced squash and pickling juice in a small saucepan and bring to a simmer. Remove from the heat, cool to room temperature, and drain off the liquid.

TO PREPARE THE SOUP: Sauté the onions with the olive oil in a medium saucepan over medium heat for 3 to 5 minutes, or until translucent. Add the chopped squash, apple, and water and bring to a simmer. Add the turmeric and cook over medium-low heat for 30 to 40 minutes, or until the squash and apple are soft. Purée the mixture until smooth. Strain through a fine-mesh sieve and season to taste with salt and pepper.

Ladle the soup into 4 shallow bowls and spoon some of the preserved squash in the center of each bowl. Sprinkle the chervil around the bowls and top with freshly ground black pepper.

> Cooking the squash in pickling juice may seem unusual, but the slightly tart diced squash makes a great flavor foil to the creamy, rich soup. Using these types of contrasts will add another level of interest to your cooking.

Mushroom-Barley Soup

SERVES 4

2 1/2 pounds button mushrooms, cleaned

1 1/2 cups chopped yellow onions

1 bulb garlic, peeled

3 sprigs thyme

5 quarts water

Salt and freshly ground black pepper

1/2 cup barley

2 roasted portobello mushrooms (see page 5)

3/4 cup roasted shiitake mushrooms (see page 5)

1 tablespoon unsalted butter

8 cloves roasted garlic, halved (see page 5)

4 teaspoons chopped fresh flat-leaf parsley

TO PREPARE THE BROTH: Place the button mushrooms, onions, garlic, thyme, and water in a large stockpot. Bring to a simmer over medium-low heat and cook for 1 1/2 hours. Strain through a coffee filter–lined sieve and discard the solids. Season the broth to taste with salt and pepper.

TO PREPARE THE BARLEY: Place the barley in a sieve and rinse with cold water for 1 minute. Place the barley in a medium saucepan with 1 1/2 cups of the mushroom broth and bring to a simmer. Cover and simmer over medium-low heat for 20 minutes, or until the barley is tender and all of the liquid has been absorbed.

MEANWHILE, PREPARE THE MUSHROOMS: Cut all the roasted mushrooms into bite-sized pieces and place in a medium sauté pan with the butter. Cook over medium heat for 5 minutes, or until warm. Season to taste with salt and pepper.

Arrange the roasted mushrooms, roasted garlic halves, and barley in the bottom of each bowl. Ladle some of the broth into each bowl, sprinkle with the parsley, and top with freshly ground black pepper.

> Mushroom broth is great to have on hand for flavoring sauces or cooking various grains. It doesn't take any longer to cook two pots of broth, so think about making a double batch and freezing the extra for use over the next several months.

Braised Leek Soup with Sautéed Oyster Mushrooms

3 large leeks (white part and
2 inches of the green)

5 cups chicken stock (see page 4)
or vegetable stock (see page 4)

2 sprigs rosemary

4 tablespoons unsalted butter

Salt and freshly ground
black pepper

1 shallot, minced

1¹/₂ cups oyster mushrooms,
cleaned

4 teaspoons extra virgin olive oil

1 tablespoon chopped fresh chives

TO PREPARE THE SOUP: Cut each leek in half lengthwise and place in a shallow pan with the stock and the rosemary. Cover and simmer over medium-low heat for 25 minutes, or until the leeks are tender. Remove and discard the rosemary. Remove the leeks and chop into bite-sized pieces. Purée two-thirds of the leeks, all of the stock, and half of the butter until smooth. Cook the soup in a medium saucepan over medium-low heat for 5 minutes, or until warm. Season to taste with salt and pepper. Keep warm. Reserve the remaining leeks for garnish.

TO PREPARE THE MUSHROOMS: Sweat the shallot in the remaining butter in a medium sauté pan over medium heat for 3 to 4 minutes, or until translucent. Add the mushrooms and cook for 5 to 7 minutes, or until tender. Season to taste with salt and pepper.

Spoon some of the mushrooms into the center of each bowl and top with the remaining leeks. Ladle the soup into the bowls and drizzle with the olive oil. Sprinkle the chives around the bowls and top with freshly ground black pepper.

> Oyster mushrooms are light in texture and flavor. If you can't find them in your grocery store, hedgehog or chanterelle mushrooms would work just as well. If these lighter varieties of mushrooms are not available, use julienned shiitake mushrooms.

Vidalia Onion Soup with Wild Rice and Maytag Blue Cheese Croutons

SERVES 4

1/2 cup wild rice

2 cups water

4 Vidalia onions, julienned

1/4 cup unsalted butter

6 cups chicken stock (see page 4) or vegetable stock (see page 4)

3 tablespoons chopped fresh basil

3 tablespoons chopped fresh chives

3 tablespoons chopped fresh tarragon

3 tablespoons chopped fresh flat-leaf parsley

Salt and freshly ground black pepper

CROUTONS

8 slices French bread

2 tablespoons extra virgin olive oil

4 ounces Maytag blue cheese

TO PREPARE THE RICE: Combine the rice and water in a medium saucepan and simmer, uncovered, over medium-low heat for 45 to 60 minutes, or until tender.

MEANWHILE, PREPARE THE SOUP: Sauté the onions with the butter in a large saucepan over medium heat for 30 to 40 minutes, or until caramelized. Add the stock and simmer for 20 minutes. Wrap the basil, chives, tarragon, and parsley in a small piece of cheesecloth and tie with kitchen string to form a sachet. Place the sachet in the onion broth and simmer for 1 minute. Remove the sachet and discard. Season to taste with salt and pepper.

TO PREPARE THE CROUTONS: Preheat the oven to 400°. Brush both sides of the bread slices with the olive oil. Place the bread on a baking sheet and toast in the oven for 12 to 15 minutes, or until light golden brown. Spread the blue cheese over the croutons while they are still warm.

Place some of the wild rice in each bowl and ladle the onion broth into the bowls. Float 2 croutons in the center of each bowl and top with freshly ground black pepper.

> Vidalia onions are grown in the sandy soil around Vidalia, Georgia. These large, sweet onions are available only in late spring and early summer. If Vidalias are out of season, Maui or yellow onions will also make a superb soup.

Roasted Garlic Soup
with Chicken Liver Croutons

SERVES 4

CROUTONS

$1/4$ cup melted unsalted butter

1 tablespoon chopped
fresh flat-leaf parsley

1 teaspoon minced garlic

8 $1/4$-inch-thick slices French bread

$1/4$ cup chopped yellow onion

$1/4$ cup chopped Granny
Smith apple

1 tablespoon canola oil

4 ounces chicken livers

Salt and freshly ground
black pepper

4 bulbs roasted garlic (see page 5),
with the cooking oil reserved

4 cups chicken stock (see page 4)

Salt and freshly ground
black pepper

TO PREPARE THE CROUTONS: Preheat the oven to 400°. Place the butter, parsley, and minced garlic in a small bowl and stir to combine. Place the bread slices on a baking sheet and brush the tops with the butter mixture. Toast in the oven for 12 to 15 minutes, or until light golden brown. Set aside.

Cook the onion and apple with the canola oil in a medium sauté pan over medium-high heat for 5 minutes, or until slightly soft. Add the chicken livers and cook, stirring occasionally, for 10 minutes, or until the livers are done. Purée the chicken liver mixture until smooth, season to taste with salt and pepper, and spread on the croutons.

TO PREPARE THE SOUP: Squeeze the garlic from the bulbs and purée with $1/4$ cup of the cooking oil and the stock until smooth. Cook the soup in a medium saucepan over medium heat for 10 minutes, or until hot. Season to taste with salt and pepper.

Ladle the soup into 4 bowls and place 2 croutons in the center of each bowl.

> Using elephant garlic in the recipe will produce a slightly sweeter, more mellow-flavored soup. For the real garlic lover, roast some extra garlic, slice, and sprinkle some in each bowl.

Lentil and Bacon Soup

1 pound bacon, julienned

1 cup diced yellow onions

1 cup diced carrots

1 cup green lentils

2 quarts chicken stock (see page 4)

Salt and freshly ground
black pepper

1/2 cup chopped scallions

TO PREPARE THE SOUP: Cook three-quarters of the bacon in a large saucepan over medium heat for 5 minutes, or until the fat is rendered. Add the onions and carrots and cook, stirring frequently, for 4 to 5 minutes, or until the onions are translucent. Drain any excess fat and add the lentils and 1 quart of the stock. Simmer over low heat for 40 to 50 minutes, or until the lentils are tender. Add the remaining stock and season to taste with salt and pepper. Cook the soup over medium heat for 10 minutes, or until hot.

TO PREPARE THE BACON: Cook the remaining bacon in a hot sauté pan over medium-high heat for 8 to 10 minutes, or until crispy. Remove the bacon from the pan and drain on paper towels.

Ladle some of the soup into each bowl and sprinkle with the crispy bacon and the scallions.

> This soup is also wonderful made with ham hocks instead of bacon. Simply cook the onions and carrots in 2 tablespoons canola oil instead of the bacon fat, and add the ham hocks with the lentils and 1 quart of stock. When the lentils are tender, remove the ham hocks from the pan and break the meat into bite-sized pieces; discard the bones and skin. Add the meat to the lentils and proceed with the recipe, omitting the garnish of crispy bacon.

salads

55 | Smoked Salmon and Potato Salad with
Scallion-Citrus Vinaigrette

56 | Smoked Salmon and Herb Salad with
Pickled Cucumber Vinaigrette

57 | Grilled Beef Tenderloin and Blue Cheese Salad

58 | Sliced Flank Steak Salad with Grilled Radicchio
and Roasted Shallot Vinaigrette

59 | Chilled Pork and Wild Rice Salad with Citrus Vinaigrette

60 | Apricot-Curry Chicken and Quinoa Salad

63 | Chilled Orzo, Asparagus, Chicken, and Goat Cheese Salad

64 | Duck Breast–Spinach Salad with Ginger-Soy Vinaigrette

65 | Israeli Couscous Salad with Spinach,
Artichokes, and Kalamata Olives

67 | Grilled Vegetable Salad with Anchovy Vinaigrette

68 | Pickled Beet and Endive Salad with Goat Cheese and Walnuts

69 | Three Bean and Potato Salad with Horseradish Vinaigrette

70 | Cantaloupe, Mango, and Asian Pear Salad with
Key Lime–Vanilla Bean Vinaigrette

72 | Shaved Fennel and Haricots Verts Salad with
Mustard Vinaigrette

Smoked Salmon and Potato Salad with Scallion-Citrus Vinaigrette

SERVES 4

12 small red potatoes

VINAIGRETTE

1/2 cup freshly squeezed orange juice

2 tablespoons freshly squeezed lime juice

2 tablespoons rice wine vinegar

3/4 cup extra virgin olive oil

1/2 cup thinly sliced scallions

Salt and freshly ground black pepper

1 apple, peeled and cored

4 cups mesclun mix (see note, page 67)

1/2 cup thinly sliced radishes

Salt and freshly ground black pepper

12 thin slices smoked salmon

TO PREPARE THE POTATOES: Place the potatoes in a large pot of salted water, bring to a boil, and cook for 20 to 25 minutes, or until tender. Cut each potato into eighths.

TO PREPARE THE VINAIGRETTE: Place the orange juice, lime juice, and vinegar in a small bowl. Whisk in the olive oil, fold in the scallions, and season to taste with salt and pepper

TO PREPARE THE SALAD: Cut the apple into 8 wedges and thinly slice widthwise. Place the apples, cooked potatoes, mesclun mix, and radishes in a mixing bowl. Toss with about half of the vinaigrette and season to taste with salt and pepper.

Place 3 slices of salmon in the center of each plate and top with some of the salad. Spoon the remaining vinaigrette around the plates and top with freshly ground black pepper.

This salad can easily be converted into smoked salmon canapés. Simply eliminate the mesclun mix and increase the amount of salmon to 24 slices. Dice the potatoes, apple, and radishes instead of slicing them and toss with half of the vinaigrette. Place some of the potato mixture at one end of each salmon slice and roll the salmon up. Cut each roll into three or four equal pieces.

Smoked Salmon and Herb Salad
with Pickled Cucumber Vinaigrette

SERVES 4

VINAIGRETTE

1/2 bay leaf

1/2 cup rice wine vinegar

1/3 cup sugar

1/2 jalapeño chile, seeded
and chopped

1/2 cup finely diced cucumber

2 tablespoons thinly sliced
red onion

3/4 teaspoon crushed
pink peppercorns

2/3 cup extra virgin olive oil

Salt and freshly ground
black pepper

1/4 cup fresh flat-leaf parsley leaves

1/4 cup fresh chervil leaves

2 tablespoons fresh
tarragon leaves

2 tablespoons fresh cilantro leaves

2 tablespoons fresh dill leaves

3 tablespoons tiny fresh
basil leaves

Salt and freshly ground
black pepper

8 ounces smoked salmon, sliced

TO PREPARE THE VINAIGRETTE: Place the bay leaf, vinegar, sugar, and jalapeño in a small saucepan and simmer over medium heat for 5 minutes. Strain through a fine-mesh sieve, discard the solids, and cool the liquid. Combine the cucumber, onion, peppercorns, and cooled vinegar mixture in a medium bowl and refrigerate until thoroughly chilled. Strain the cucumber mixture, reserving 1/4 cup of the liquid. In a small bowl, whisk together the reserved cucumber liquid and the olive oil. Add the cucumber mixture to the liquid and season to taste with salt and pepper.

TO PREPARE THE SALAD: Place all of the herbs in a medium bowl and toss with 3 tablespoons of the vinaigrette. Season to taste with salt and pepper.

TO PREPARE THE SALMON: Cut the salmon slices into 1/4-inch-wide strips and toss with 2 tablespoons of the vinaigrette.

Arrange some of the herb salad in the center of each plate and top with a mound of the salmon. Spoon the remaining vinaigrette around the plates and top with freshly ground black pepper.

> Pink peppercorns can be hard to find and they aren't cheap, but they provide a flavor and heat that is difficult to match. If you can't find them, don't despair. A small seeded and finely minced Thai chile (see note, page 19) can be substituted for this recipe.

Grilled Beef Tenderloin and Blue Cheese Salad

SERVES 4

VINAIGRETTE

1 shallot, minced

$1/3$ cup freshly squeezed lemon juice

2 tablespoons chopped fresh chives

1 tablespoon chopped fresh flat-leaf parsley

1 cup extra virgin olive oil

Salt and freshly ground black pepper

12 ounces beef tenderloin

Salt and freshly ground black pepper

6 cups baby spinach leaves, cleaned

$1^1/3$ cups crumbled blue cheese

TO PREPARE THE VINAIGRETTE: Place the shallot, lemon juice, chives, and parsley in a small bowl. Slowly whisk in the olive oil and season to taste with salt and pepper.

TO PREPARE THE BEEF: Prepare a medium-hot grill. Season the beef with salt and pepper and grill for 4 to 5 minutes on each side, or until cooked to desired doneness. Cool completely and dice into $1/2$-inch pieces. Toss with 3 tablespoons of the vinaigrette and season to taste with salt and pepper.

TO PREPARE THE GREENS: Toss the spinach with half of the remaining vinaigrette and half of the blue cheese. Season to taste with salt and pepper.

Place some of the spinach in the center of each plate. Arrange the beef and the remaining blue cheese on the salad and drizzle the remaining vinaigrette around the plates. Top with freshly ground black pepper.

> For a richer, more intensely flavored vinaigrette, substitute balsamic vinegar (see note, page 130) for the lemon juice and omit the parsley.

Sliced Flank Steak Salad with Grilled Radicchio and Roasted Shallot Vinaigrette

SERVES 4

VINAIGRETTE

4 shallots, peeled

3/4 cup extra virgin olive oil

3 tablespoons balsamic vinegar (see note, page 130)

2 tablespoons chopped fresh chives

Salt and freshly ground black pepper

2 heads radicchio, quartered

1 tablespoon plus 1/4 cup extra virgin olive oil

Salt and freshly ground black pepper

4 4-ounce pieces flank steak

2 sprigs thyme

TO PREPARE THE VINAIGRETTE: Preheat the oven to 350°. Place the shallots and olive oil in a small ovenproof pan and cover tightly. Bake for 50 to 60 minutes, or until the shallots are soft. Remove from the oven and let the shallots cool in the olive oil, and then remove them, reserving the oil. Julienne the shallots and put them in a medium bowl. Add the balsamic vinegar and slowly whisk in the reserved olive oil. Add the chives and season to taste with salt and pepper.

TO PREPARE THE RADICCHIO: Prepare a medium grill. Brush the radicchio with the 1 tablespoon olive oil and season to taste with salt and pepper. Grill for 5 to 7 minutes, or until wilted. Coarsely chop and season to taste with salt and pepper.

TO PREPARE THE STEAK: Season the flank steak with salt and pepper and rub with the 1/4 cup olive oil. Remove the thyme leaves from the stems, rub them onto the beef, and grill for 5 to 7 minutes on each side, or until medium-rare. Let rest for 3 minutes and cut each steak into 1/4-inch-thick slices on the diagonal.

Place some of the radicchio in the center of each plate. Arrange the sliced flank steak over the radicchio, and spoon the vinaigrette over the steak. Top with freshly ground black pepper.

> Grilling lettuce may seem unusual, but the peppery flavor and firm texture of radicchio lends itself perfectly to this cooking method. Grilling the radicchio adds an extra flavor dimension that helps it stand up to the steak.

Chilled Pork and Wild Rice Salad
with Citrus Vinaigrette

SERVES 4

2 thick-cut boneless pork chops
(6 to 8 ounces each)

Salt and freshly ground
black pepper

2 tablespoons canola oil

1 cup wild rice

4 cups water

1/2 cup chopped dried apricots

1/4 cup freshly squeezed
orange juice

VINAIGRETTE

1 tablespoon cumin seeds

4 1/2 tablespoons raspberry vinegar

1/2 cup plus 2 tablespoons
extra virgin olive oil

Salt and freshly ground
black pepper

1/4 cup finely minced red onion

2 cups watercress, stemmed

1/2 cup walnuts, toasted
(see note, page 36)
and chopped

TO PREPARE THE PORK: Season the pork chops with salt and pepper. Heat the canola oil in a hot sauté pan over high heat and sear the pork chops for 2 to 3 minutes on each side, or until golden brown. Decrease the heat to medium, cover, and cook for 5 to 7 minutes, or until done. Refrigerate the meat for 1 hour.

MEANWHILE, PREPARE THE RICE: Combine the rice and water in a saucepan and simmer over medium-low heat for 45 to 60 minutes, or until tender.

TO PREPARE THE APRICOTS: Place the apricots in the orange juice and let stand at room temperature for 20 minutes.

TO PREPARE THE VINAIGRETTE: Place the cumin seeds in a small sauté pan over medium heat and toast for 3 minutes, or until they give off a strong aroma. Coarsely grind the cumin in a spice or coffee grinder or with a mortar and pestle. Place the cumin and raspberry vinegar in a small bowl and whisk in the olive oil. Season to taste with salt and pepper.

TO PREPARE THE SALAD: Thinly slice the pork and toss in a bowl with 1/2 cup of the vinaigrette. Combine the onion, rice, watercress, walnuts, apricots, and the remaining vinaigrette in a large bowl, toss well, and season with salt and pepper.

Place some of the salad in the center of each plate and top with the pork slices.

This dish can easily be made up to 1 day ahead. To serve it family style, cut the pork into bite-sized pieces and mix into the salad.

Apricot-Curry Chicken and Quinoa Salad

**SERVES 4 AS APPETIZER,
SERVES 2 AS ENTRÉE**

SAUCE

3/4 cup dried apricots

3/4 teaspoon hot curry powder
(see note, page 30)

1/4 cup rice wine vinegar

1/2 cup water

QUINOA

2 cups water

1 teaspoon canola oil

1 cup quinoa

2 teaspoons canola oil

2 boneless, skinless chicken
breasts

3 tablespoons extra virgin olive oil

3 tablespoons freshly squeezed
orange juice

1/2 cup diced cucumber

1/4 cup finely diced red bell pepper

Salt and freshly ground
black pepper

1/4 cup thinly sliced dried apricot

2 teaspoons finely chopped
fresh chives

TO PREPARE THE SAUCE: Purée the apricots with the curry powder, vinegar, and water until smooth. Strain through a fine-mesh sieve and refrigerate for at least 1 hour, or until ready to use.

TO PREPARE THE QUINOA: Bring the water to a boil in a medium saucepan. Meanwhile, heat the canola oil in a medium sauté pan over medium heat. Add the quinoa and cook, stirring frequently, for 5 minutes, or until it has a nutty aroma. Stir the quinoa into the boiling water and bring to a simmer. Cover and cook over medium-low heat for 15 minutes, or until most of the liquid is absorbed. Remove from the heat, cover tightly, and let stand for 15 minutes.

TO PREPARE THE CHICKEN: Heat the canola oil in a small sauté pan over medium heat. Add the chicken and cook, turning once, for 5 minutes, or until lightly browned. Add one-quarter of the apricot sauce, cover, and cook over medium-low heat for 10 to 15 minutes, or until the chicken is done. Thinly slice the chicken into bite-sized pieces.

continued

Quinoa is an amazing grain that is just starting to become more popular in the United States. It is often called the super-grain because it comes closer than any other food to providing all of the nutrients needed to sustain life. It has a crumbly, light texture with a slight crunch. It may take a little hunting to find it, but the flavor, texture, and nutritional value make it well worth the effort. You can purchase apricot-curry sauce at www.charlietrotters.com.

TO PREPARE THE SALAD: Mix the quinoa, olive oil, orange juice, cucumber, bell pepper, and chicken with the remaining apricot sauce and season to taste with salt and pepper. Refrigerate for 1 hour, or until ready to serve.

TO PREPARE AS AN ENTRÉE: Use chicken breasts with skin and cook as directed above, but do not slice. Prepare the salad as directed, but do not add the chicken and use only half of the remaining apricot sauce. To serve two, mound half of the quinoa salad on a plate, and top with chicken breast. Drizzle some of the remaining apricot sauce around the plate and garnish with dried apricot slices and chopped chives.

Chilled Orzo, Asparagus, Chicken, and Goat Cheese Salad

SERVES 4

1 teaspoon canola oil

1 boneless, skinless chicken breast

1 cup orzo

2¹/₂ tablespoons balsamic vinegar (see note, page 130)

¹/₂ cup extra virgin olive oil

15 asparagus spears, trimmed, sliced on the diagonal, and parboiled

4 ounces soft goat cheese (see note, page 35), crumbled

Salt and freshly ground black pepper

¹/₄ cup pine nuts, toasted (see note, page 36)

TO PREPARE THE CHICKEN: Heat the canola oil in a small sauté pan over medium heat, add the chicken, and cook for 5 minutes on each side, or until done. Cool and cut into bite-sized pieces.

TO PREPARE THE SALAD: Bring a large pot of salted water to a boil. Add the orzo and cook for 7 minutes, or until al dente. Pour the orzo into a strainer and run under cold water for 1 minute. Whisk together the vinegar and olive oil in a large bowl and stir in the orzo. Refrigerate until chilled.

Stir in the chicken, asparagus, and goat cheese and season to taste with salt and pepper. Refrigerate until ready to serve. Stir in the pine nuts just prior to serving.

> Orzo is a small, oval-shaped pasta that is readily available in most grocery stores. It comes in various sizes, but the largest variety would be best for this salad.

Duck Breast–Spinach Salad with Ginger-Soy Vinaigrette

VINAIGRETTE

1 tablespoon peeled and minced fresh ginger

2 tablespoons soy sauce

2 tablespoons rice wine vinegar

³/₄ cup sesame oil

4 small duck breasts, trimmed and skin scored

Salt and freshly ground black pepper

4 cups baby spinach leaves, cleaned

1 cup sliced button mushrooms

TO PREPARE THE VINAIGRETTE: Combine all of the ingredients for the vinaigrette in a small saucepan. Cook over low heat for 5 minutes, or until warm.

TO PREPARE THE DUCK: Season the duck breasts with salt and pepper and place in a very hot sauté pan over high heat with the skin side down first. Cook for 3 to 4 minutes on each side, or until the skin is golden brown and crispy and the duck is cooked medium. Remove the duck from the pan, let rest for 2 minutes, and slice on the diagonal.

TO PREPARE THE SPINACH: Place the spinach leaves in a large bowl, toss with half of the warm vinaigrette, and season to taste with salt and pepper.

Place a bed of spinach leaves in the center of each plate and top with the mushrooms. Arrange the warm duck slices in the center of the spinach and spoon the remaining vinaigrette over the duck. Top with freshly ground black pepper.

> Duck breasts are wonderful, but if you have never cooked them before, you will quickly learn that they are very fatty. Don't be afraid to trim any visible fat; there is plenty more you can't see. The keys to cooking duck breasts are scoring the skin, which helps to drain off excess fat; making sure the pan is very hot before adding the duck; and cooking the duck skin side down first. These steps ensure a crispy skin and will render the fat from the duck.

Israeli Couscous Salad with Spinach, Artichokes, and Kalamata Olives

SERVES 6

ARTICHOKES

¼ cup peeled and diced carrot

½ cup diced yellow onion

¼ cup diced celery

2 tablespoons unsalted butter

3 artichokes, stem trimmed, top half and leaves removed

½ lemon

COUSCOUS

1½ cups raw Israeli couscous

3 tablespoons extra virgin olive oil

VINAIGRETTE

¼ cup freshly squeezed lemon juice

5 tablepoons extra virgin olive oil

Salt and freshly ground black pepper

Salt and freshly ground black pepper

2 cups baby spinach leaves, cleaned and chopped

1 cup kalamata olives, pitted and coarsely chopped

TO PREPARE THE ARTICHOKES: Cook the carrot, onion, and celery in the butter in a medium saucepan over medium-low heat for 5 minutes, or until the onion is translucent. Add the artichoke bottoms and lemon and cover with water. Simmer over medium heat for 20 to 25 minutes, or until the artichokes are done. Remove the artichokes from the pan, scoop out the grassy centers, and discard. Cool the artichokes to room temperature.

TO PREPARE THE COUSCOUS: Place the couscous in a sieve and rinse with cold water. Place in a large pot of salted water and bring to a boil. Cook over medium heat, stirring occasionally, for 12 to 15 minutes, or until al dente. Pour the couscous into a strainer and rinse with cold water for 3 minutes. Drain, place in a large bowl, and toss with the olive oil.

TO PREPARE THE VINAIGRETTE: Whisk together the lemon juice and olive oil in a small bowl and season to taste with salt and pepper.

TO PREPARE THE SALAD: Slice the artichokes in half, cut into small wedges, and season to taste with salt and pepper. Add the artichokes, spinach, olives, and vinaigrette to the couscous and toss well. Refrigerate for at least 1 hour before serving to allow the flavors to meld.

Israeli couscous (sometimes called Middle Eastern couscous) is much larger than regular couscous and has a chewier texture. It lends itself well to use in cold salads because it retains its texture even when mixed with vinaigrettes or sauces. Look for it in gourmet markets or health food stores.

Grilled Vegetable Salad
with Anchovy Vinaigrette

SERVES 4

VINAIGRETTE

2 tablespoons anchovy paste

2 tablespoons freshly
squeezed lemon juice

$1/2$ cup extra virgin olive oil

Salt and freshly ground
black pepper

VEGETABLES

1 zucchini, sliced lengthwise
$1/8$ inch thick

1 yellow squash, sliced
lengthwise $1/8$ inch thick

1 small eggplant, sliced
lengthwise $1/4$ inch thick

$1/4$ cup extra virgin olive oil

Salt and freshly ground
black pepper

1 roasted red bell pepper (see
page 5), cut into 1-inch pieces

4 cups mesclun mix

$1/2$ cup mizuna

2 tablespoons pine nuts,
toasted (see note, page 36)

2 tablespoons coarsely
chopped anchovy pieces

2 tablespoons shaved
Parmesan cheese

Freshly ground black pepper

TO PREPARE THE VINAIGRETTE: Whisk together the anchovy paste, lemon juice, and olive oil in a small bowl and season to taste with salt and pepper.

TO PREPARE THE VEGETABLES: Prepare a medium-hot grill. Rub the zucchini, yellow squash, and eggplant with the olive oil and season to taste with salt and pepper. Grill the vegetables for 2 minutes on each side, or until cooked. Remove from the grill and cut into bite-sized pieces. Add the red bell pepper and season to taste with salt and pepper.

TO PREPARE THE GREENS: Place the mesclun and mizuna in a large bowl and toss with $1/2$ cup of the vinaigrette. Season to taste with salt and pepper.

Place some of the greens in the center of each plate and top with some of the grilled vegetables. Drizzle the remaining vinaigrette over the vegetables, sprinkle with the pine nuts, anchovy pieces, and Parmesan cheese. Top with freshly ground black pepper.

> Mesclun mix is a combination of several tender baby lettuces, usually baby spinach, red oak leaf, and frisée. It is usually sold in the bulk section of the produce department in grocery stores, but it is also sometimes available in small packages labeled "gourmet mix." If your grocery store does not carry it, any combination of tender baby lettuces will work fine.

Pickled Beet and Endive Salad with Goat Cheese and Walnuts

SERVES 4

VINAIGRETTE

1 shallot, minced

$1/3$ cup sherry wine vinegar

$1/2$ cup canola oil

$1/2$ cup extra virgin olive oil

Salt and freshly ground
black pepper

2 beets

2 cups pickling juice (see page 6)

Salt and freshly ground
black pepper

20 small Belgian endive leaves

1 pear, peeled, cored, and
thinly sliced

1 cup soft goat cheese (see note,
page 35), crumbled

$3/4$ cup walnuts, toasted (see note,
page 36) and coarsely chopped

Salt and freshly ground
black pepper

TO PREPARE THE VINAIGRETTE: Place the shallot and vinegar in a small bowl and slowly whisk in the canola and olive oils. Season to taste with salt and pepper.

TO PREPARE THE BEETS: Place the beets in a small saucepan with salted water. Bring to a boil and cook for 15 to 20 minutes, or until tender. Drain the beets, cool slightly, and peel. Julienne the beets and place them in a medium bowl with the pickling juice for 2 hours. Drain, discarding the pickling juice. Toss with 2 tablespoons of the vinaigrette and season to taste with salt and pepper.

TO PREPARE THE SALAD: In a large bowl, toss the endive, pear, goat cheese, and walnuts with the remaining vinaigrette and season to taste with salt and pepper.

Arrange some of the salad in the center of each plate and top with the beets. Top with freshly ground black pepper.

> Belgian endive is a crisp, slightly bitter lettuce with white and yellow leaves. Belgian endive and beets are a perfect study in contrasts: The sweet, tender beets offset the slightly bitter, crispy endive, and the color contrasts are stunning.

Three Bean and Potato Salad
with Horseradish Vinaigrette

SERVES 6

1 pound fingerling potatoes or other small white potatoes

VINAIGRETTE

¼ cup grated fresh horseradish

¼ cup rice wine vinegar

3 tablespoons freshly squeezed lemon juice

¾ cup extra virgin olive oil

Salt and freshly ground black pepper

1 cup cooked navy beans

1 cup cooked scarlet runner beans

1 cup cooked kidney beans

½ cup thinly sliced red onion

½ cup thinly sliced celery

3 tablespoons chopped fresh flat-leaf parsley

3 tablespoons chopped fresh chives

Salt and freshly ground black pepper

TO PREPARE THE POTATOES: Place the potatoes in a large pot of salted water and bring to a boil. Cook for 20 to 25 minutes, or until tender. Drain the potatoes, cool to room temperature, and cut them into bite-sized pieces.

TO PREPARE THE VINAIGRETTE: Whisk together the horseradish, vinegar, lemon juice, and olive oil in a small bowl and season to taste with salt and pepper.

TO PREPARE THE SALAD: Combine the potatoes, navy beans, scarlet runner beans, kidney beans, onion, celery, parsley, and chives in a large bowl. Toss with the vinaigrette and season to taste with salt and pepper. Refrigerate for at least 1 hour before serving to meld the flavors.

This salad works well with any type of dried beans. Keep in mind, however, that most of the color in the dish comes from the beans, and a variety of colors will look more appealing.

Dried beans should always be soaked for at least 12 hours in cold water before using to ensure even cooking. Beans are best when cooked at a very slow simmer with water and a few tablespoons of butter, or, if you are avoiding fat, in chicken stock. The butter or stock will add a wonderful richness to the beans.

Cantaloupe, Mango, and Asian Pear Salad with Key Lime–Vanilla Bean Vinaigrette

SERVES 4

VINAIGRETTE

3 tablespoons freshly squeezed key lime juice

Pulp of 1 vanilla bean

1/4 cup plus 3 tablespoons extra virgin olive oil

Salt and freshly ground black pepper

1 cup large-diced cantaloupe

1 cup large-diced mango

1 cup large-diced Asian pear, sliced into sticks

1/4 cup thinly sliced red onion

1 teaspoon key lime zest, finely sliced

1 cup watercress, stemmed

1 teaspoon fresh frosted or common mint leaves

TO PREPARE THE VINAIGRETTE: Whisk together the lime juice, vanilla bean pulp, and olive oil in a small bowl. Season to taste with salt and pepper.

TO PREPARE THE SALAD: Combine cantaloupe, mango, pear, onion, and lime zest in a large bowl and toss with the vinaigrette. Refrigerate for at least 1 hour before serving. Toss with the watercress and garnish with mint just prior to serving.

> Key limes are small, round limes with a slightly sweet, slightly floral flavor. They are available in the produce department of many grocery stores, but if you aren't able to find them, regular Persian limes will do.

Shaved Fennel and Haricots Verts Salad with Mustard Vinaigrette

SERVES 4

VINAIGRETTE

3 tablespoons whole-grain mustard

3 tablespoons freshly squeezed lemon juice

$3/4$ cup extra virgin olive oil

Salt and freshly ground black pepper

3 cups very thinly sliced fennel

20 haricots verts or green beans, parboiled

Salt and freshly ground black pepper

TO PREPARE THE VINAIGRETTE: In a small bowl, whisk together the mustard, lemon juice, and olive oil until smooth and season to taste with salt and pepper.

TO PREPARE THE SALAD: In a large bowl, toss the fennel and haricots verts with the vinaigrette and season to taste with salt and pepper. Refrigerate for at least 1 hour before serving.

This salad can be made into an appetizer or an entrée by serving it in individual plates topped with a piece of poached salmon.

ENTRÉES

seafood | poultry | meat | vegetables

seafood

76 | Peppered Tuna with Wild Mushroom Ragout

78 | Cilantro-Crusted Tuna Loin with Bok Choy and
Lemon-Sesame Vinaigrette

79 | Grilled Tuna Steak with Quinoa and Roasted
Shallot Vinaigrette

81 | Sautéed Sea Bass with Roasted White Eggplant
and Black Olive Purées

82 | Steamed Sea Bass with Yukon Gold Potato Purée
and Asparagus

83 | Sautéed Sweet and Sour Cod with Oyster Mushrooms
and Somen Noodles

85 | Olive Oil–Poached Cod with Roasted Tomatoes
and Broccoli Rabe

86 | Grilled Catfish with Yellow Tomato Sauce and Scallions

87 | Sautéed Catfish with Caramelized Onion Risotto

88 | Slow-Roasted Salmon with Garlic and Thyme Risotto

90 | Cold-Poached Salmon with Shaved Fennel and Apple Salad

91 | Grilled Salmon Steaks with Marinated Tomatoes
     and Eggplant

92 | Sautéed Snapper with Caramelized Onion–Strewn Grits
     and Red Wine Pan Sauce

93 | Ponzu-Marinated Scallops with Daikon and Bok Choy

95 | Grilled Scallop and Red Onion Brochettes

96 | Lobster Tail with Horseradish Potatoes and Haricots Verts

99 | Grilled Shrimp and Vegetables with Linguine

100 | Sautéed Sea Scallops with Wild Mushroom Stew

101 | Panko-and-Horseradish-Crusted Shrimp with Miso Broth

102 | Herb-Crusted Halibut with Roasted Potatoes and
      Shiitake Mushroom Sauce

103 | Grilled Halibut with Warm Tomato and Roasted
      Garlic Salad

104 | Fettuccine and Spinach in Saffron-Mussel Broth

Peppered Tuna with
Wild Mushroom Ragout

SERVES 4

RAGOUT

1 large shallot, finely diced

1 tablespoon unsalted butter

3 cups mixed roasted mushrooms (see page 5), with the cooking liquid reserved

Salt and freshly ground black pepper

1 pound sashimi-grade tuna loin

2 tablespoons extra virgin olive oil

2 teaspoons coarsely ground black pepper

$1/2$ cup meat stock reduction (see page 4)

1 tablespoon fresh tiny thyme shoots (soft thyme)

$1/2$ teaspoon green peppercorns, coarsely ground

$1/2$ teaspoon red peppercorns, coarsely ground

TO PREPARE THE RAGOUT: Cook the shallot in the butter in a large sauté pan over medium heat for 3 to 4 minutes, or until translucent but not brown. Add the mushrooms and cook for 3 minutes, or until warm. Season to taste with salt and pepper.

TO PREPARE THE TUNA: Cut the tuna lengthwise into 2 pieces. Rub the pieces with 1 tablespoon of the olive oil, and coat with the pepper. Heat the remaining 1 tablespoon olive oil in a medium sauté pan over medium-high heat and sauté the tuna on all sides for 3 to 5 minutes total. The tuna should still be quite raw in the center. Remove the tuna from the pan and cut crosswise into $1/4$-inch-thick slices.

TO PREPARE THE SAUCE: Heat the meat stock reduction and $1/4$ cup of the roasted mushroom liquid in a small saucepan over medium heat for 5 minutes, or until warm.

Spoon some of the mushrooms in the center of each plate. Layer the tuna slices in an overlapping pattern on top of the mushrooms, and spoon the sauce over the tuna and around the plate. Sprinkle the thyme and red and green peppercorns around the plates.

> It is essential to use sashimi-grade tuna whenever tuna is left even partially raw. If you cannot find sashimi-grade tuna in a reputable fish market, prepare this recipe with salmon instead.

Cilantro-Crusted Tuna Loin with Bok Choy and Lemon-Sesame Vinaigrette

SERVES 4

VINAIGRETTE

$1/4$ cup freshly squeezed lemon juice

1 tablespoon rice wine vinegar

3 tablespoons sesame oil

5 tablespoons canola oil

Salt and freshly ground black pepper

1 head bok choy, sliced

4 4-ounce pieces sashimi-grade tuna loin (see note, page 76)

2 tablespoon canola oil

Salt and freshly ground black pepper

$1/3$ cup finely chopped fresh cilantro

TO PREPARE THE VINAIGRETTE: Combine the lemon juice and vinegar in a small bowl and whisk in the sesame and canola oils. Season to taste with salt and pepper.

TO PREPARE THE BOK CHOY: Heat $1/4$ cup of the vinaigrette in a large sauté pan over medium heat. Add the bok choy and cook for 6 to 8 minutes, or until the bok choy is just cooked.

TO PREPARE THE TUNA: Rub the tuna with 1 tablespoon of the canola oil, season with salt and pepper, and coat with the cilantro. Place the remaining 1 tablespoon canola oil in a hot sauté pan over high heat and quickly sear each side of the tuna for 1 minute, or until golden brown. The tuna should still be quite raw in the center. Slice each piece in half on the diagonal and season the inside flesh with salt and pepper.

Spoon some of the bok choy in the center of each plate and top with 2 pieces of tuna. Spoon the remaining vinaigrette over the tuna and around the plates.

> Bok choy is a Chinese cabbage that is available in most grocery stores. If you can find it, baby bok choy will make this dish a little more visually interesting. If baby bok choy is available, buy 4 heads, cook them whole, and place one in the center of each plate instead of the chopped bok choy.

Grilled Tuna Steak with Quinoa and Roasted Shallot Vinaigrette

SERVES 4

VINAIGRETTE

4 large shallots, peeled

3/4 cup extra virgin olive oil

3 tablespoons balsamic vinegar (see note, page 130)

2 tablespoons chopped fresh chives

Salt and freshly ground black pepper

QUINOA

2 cups water

1 teaspoon canola oil

1 cup quinoa (see note, page 60)

4 5-ounce tuna steaks

1 small eggplant, sliced 1/2 inch thick

2 tablespoons extra virgin olive oil

Salt and freshly ground black pepper

TO PREPARE THE VINAIGRETTE: Preheat the oven to 350°. Place the shallots and olive oil in a small roasting pan and cover tightly. Bake for 50 to 60 minutes, or until the shallots are soft. Let the shallots cool in the olive oil and then remove the shallots, reserving the oil. Julienne the shallots and put them in a medium bowl. Add the vinegar and slowly whisk in the reserved olive oil. Add the chives and season to taste with salt and pepper.

TO PREPARE THE QUINOA: Bring the water to a boil in a medium saucepan. Meanwhile, heat the canola oil in a medium sauté pan over medium heat. Add the quinoa and cook, stirring frequently, for 5 minutes, or until it has a nutty aroma. Stir the quinoa into the boiling water and bring to a simmer. Cover and cook over medium-low heat for 15 minutes, or until most of the liquid is absorbed. Remove from the heat, cover tightly, and let stand for 15 minutes.

continued

This is a great dish for a casual summer barbecue. The vinaigrette can be prepared in advance and refrigerated (warm it to room temperature before serving), and the remaining ingredients—the tuna steaks, the eggplant, and the quinoa—require very little cooking time, allowing plenty of time for good conversation. Toasting the quinoa in the canola oil is an extra step, but it doesn't take much time, and it does intensify the natural nut flavor present in this protein-rich South American grain.

TO PREPARE THE TUNA AND EGGPLANT: Prepare a medium-hot grill. Rub the tuna steaks and eggplant with the olive oil and season with salt and pepper. Grill the tuna steaks and eggplant for 2 to 3 minutes on each side, or until the tuna is cooked medium-rare and the eggplant is tender.

Dice the eggplant, toss with the quinoa and $1/2$ cup of the vinaigrette, and season to taste with salt and pepper.

Place some of the quinoa in the center of each plate and top with a tuna steak. Spoon the remaining vinaigrette over the tuna steaks and around the plates.

Sautéed Sea Bass with Roasted White Eggplant and Black Olive Purées

SERVES 4

2 small white eggplants, peeled and cut into large dice

1 teaspoon salt, plus more to taste

2 tablespoons extra virgin olive oil

Freshly ground black pepper

2 tablespoons chopped basil

1 cup plus 6 whole kalamata olives, pitted

4 5-ounce sea bass fillets, skinned

1 tablespoon canola oil

TO PREPARE THE EGGPLANT PURÉE: Place the eggplant in a medium bowl and toss with the 1 teaspoon salt. Let stand at room temperature for 30 minutes. Preheat the oven to 400°. Place the eggplant in a sieve and rinse with water to remove the salt. Drain thoroughly and place on a rimmed baking sheet. Toss the eggplant with the olive oil, spread the eggplant evenly on the pan, and add $1/2$ inch of water to the pan. Roast for 40 to 50 minutes, or until tender. Purée half of the eggplant, adding a little of the cooking liquid if necessary, until smooth. Season to taste with salt and pepper. Toss the remaining eggplant with 1 tablespoon of the basil and season to taste with salt and pepper.

TO PREPARE THE OLIVE PURÉE: Purée the 1 cup of olives, adding their juice as needed to create a smooth purée. Cut the remaining olives into thin wedges.

TO PREPARE THE BASS: Season both sides of the bass fillets with salt and pepper. Quickly sauté in a hot sauté pan over medium-high heat with the canola oil for 1 to 2 minutes on each side, or until done.

Spoon a large circle of eggplant purée in the center of each plate, spoon on the diced eggplant, and top with a piece of bass. Spoon the olive purée over the fish and around the plates. Sprinkle the olive wedges and the remaining 1 tablespoon basil around the plates.

White eggplant is slightly more bitter than regular eggplant and stands up well to the olive purée. If you can't find white eggplant, use regular eggplant instead.

Steamed Sea Bass with Yukon Gold Potato Purée and Asparagus

SERVES 4

POTATO PURÉE

2 pounds Yukon Gold potatoes, peeled and quartered

Salt and freshly ground black pepper

$1/2$ cup milk

2 tablespoons unsalted butter

1 cup julienned yellow onions

1 tablespoon unsalted butter

VINAIGRETTE

3 tablespoons freshly squeezed lemon juice

$1/3$ cup extra virgin olive oil

1 tablespoon chopped fresh chives

Salt and freshly ground black pepper

4 5-ounce sea bass fillets, skinned

Salt and freshly ground black pepper

3 tablespoons chopped fresh chives

$1^1/2$ tablespoons chopped fresh chervil

1 pound asparagus spears, trimmed, sliced on the diagonal, and parboiled

TO PREPARE THE POTATOES: Place the potatoes in a large pot of salted water and bring to a boil. Cook for 15 to 20 minutes, or until tender. Drain the water, add the milk and butter to the pot, and bring to a full boil over high heat. Remove from the heat and whip with an electric mixer or hand masher until smooth. Season to taste with salt and pepper, cover, and keep warm.

TO PREPARE THE ONIONS: Cook the onion with the butter in a small sauté pan over medium-high heat for 15 minutes, or until caramelized.

TO PREPARE THE VINAIGRETTE: In a small bowl, whisk together the lemon juice, olive oil, and chives. Season to taste with salt and pepper.

TO PREPARE THE SEA BASS: Bring water to a boil in a steamer. Season both sides of the bass with salt and pepper. Press the chives and chervil on top of the fish to form a crust. Place the bass on the steamer rack, cover, and steam for 3 minutes, or until just cooked.

TO PREPARE THE ASPARAGUS: Place the asparagus in a medium bowl and toss with 2 tablespoons of the vinaigrette.

Spoon some of the potatoes into the center of each plate and top with some of the onions. Place a piece of bass over the onions. Arrange the asparagus around the plate and drizzle the remaining vinaigrette over the fish and around the plate.

> If you don't have a steamer, you can place a cake cooling rack in the bottom of any pan that has a cover and is large enough to fit your rack. When steaming fish, make sure the water does not touch the fish or it will dilute the flavor.

Sautéed Sweet and Sour Cod with Oyster Mushrooms and Somen Noodles

SERVES 4

¹/₄ cup sugar

¹/₄ cup rice wine vinegar

2 tablespoons soy sauce

1 jalapeño chile, seeded and finely chopped

4 5-ounce cod fillets

Salt and freshly ground black pepper

¹/₄ cup sesame oil

2 cups oyster mushrooms, cleaned, stemmed, and cut into bite-sized pieces

2 tablespoons unsalted butter

8 ounces dried somen noodles

¹/₂ cup chopped scallions

¹/₄ cup fresh basil leaves, cut into thin strips (see note, page 24)

TO PREPARE THE COD: Combine the sugar, vinegar, soy sauce, and jalapeño in a small saucepan over medium heat and simmer for 3 minutes. Remove from the heat and cool.

Season the cod with salt and pepper and brush thoroughly with the sugar mixture. Heat 1 tablespoon of the sesame oil in a large sauté pan over medium heat. Add the cod and cook for 3 to 4 minutes on each side, or until slightly underdone. Remove from the heat and keep warm.

TO PREPARE THE MUSHROOMS: Cook the mushrooms in the butter in a medium sauté pan over medium heat for 5 to 7 minutes, or until tender. Season to taste with salt and pepper.

TO PREPARE THE NOODLES: Bring a large pot of salted water to a boil. Add the noodles and cook over medium heat for 6 to 8 minutes, or until al dente. Drain, and toss the warm noodles with the remaining 3 tablespoons sesame oil, the scallions, and basil.

Place some of the noodles in the center of each plate. Spoon the mushrooms on the noodles and top with a piece of cod.

> Somen noodles are thin, white Japanese noodles made from wheat flour. They are available in the Asian section of most grocery stores, but if you can't find them, vermicelli can be used instead.

Olive Oil–Poached Cod with Roasted Tomatoes and Broccoli Rabe

SERVES 4

TOMATOES

3 large tomatoes

3 cloves garlic

1/2 cup extra virgin olive oil

1/4 cup balsamic vinegar
(see note, page 130)

2 sprigs thyme

Salt and freshly ground
black pepper

1 bunch broccoli rabe,
cleaned and blanched

2 tablespoons unsalted butter

Salt and freshly ground
black pepper

2 cups plus 1 tablespoon
extra virgin olive oil

4 5-ounce cod fillets, skinned

1 teaspoon fresh tiny green
basil leaves

1 teaspoon fresh tiny purple
basil leaves

TO PREPARE THE TOMATOES: Preheat the oven to 375°. Bring a large pot of water to a boil. Blanch the tomatoes in the boiling water for 30 seconds and then peel off the skins. Cut each tomato into 8 wedges, place in a small roasting pan, and toss lightly with the garlic, olive oil, balsamic vinegar, and thyme. Bake for 20 to 25 minutes, or until the tomatoes are soft. Remove the tomatoes from the pan, season to taste with salt and pepper, and keep warm. Strain the cooking liquid through a fine-mesh sieve and season to taste with salt and pepper. Keep warm.

TO PREPARE THE BROCCOLI RABE: Cook the broccoli rabe in the butter in a small sauté pan over medium heat for 5 minutes, or until warm. Season to taste with salt and pepper.

TO PREPARE THE COD: Warm the 2 cups olive oil in a medium saucepan over a very low flame to 110°. Season both sides of the fish with salt and pepper and place in the warm oil. The oil should cover the fish. Cook for 3 minutes, turn the fish over, and cook for an additional 3 minutes, or until just done.

Place some of the roasted tomatoes in the center of each plate and top with a piece of fish. Arrange the broccoli rabe around the plate and drizzle the tomato cooking liquid and the 1 tablespoon olive oil over the fish and around the plate. Garnish with tiny green and purple basil.

Poaching in oil may sound like it would produce oil-soaked fish, but it actually seals in the juices and results in tender, moist fillets. It is a good cooking technique for firmer fish such as cod, swordfish, or salmon. The key is for the oil to be warm, but not hot. Keep the thermometer in the oil as the fish is cooking, and adjust the heat to maintain a temperature of 110° to 115°. If you cannot find broccoli rabe, you may substitute one small head of broccoli.

Grilled Catfish with
Yellow Tomato Sauce and Scallions

SERVES 4

SAUCE

1 large yellow onion, diced

2 cloves garlic, chopped

2 tablespoons unsalted butter

3 yellow tomatoes, coarsely chopped

Salt and freshly ground black pepper

4 5-ounce catfish fillets, skinned

3 tablespoons extra virgin olive oil

Salt and freshly ground black pepper

16 scallions, cleaned and trimmed

TO PREPARE THE SAUCE: Cook the onion and garlic in the butter in a medium sauté pan over medium heat for 5 minutes, or until the onion is translucent. Add the tomatoes and cook for 20 to 30 minutes, or until most of the liquid from the tomatoes is reduced. Purée the tomatoes until smooth, season to taste with salt and pepper, and keep warm.

TO PREPARE THE CATFISH: Prepare a medium-hot grill. Rub the catfish with 2 tablespoons of the olive oil and season both sides with salt and pepper. Grill for 3 to 4 minutes on each side, or until done.

TO PREPARE THE SCALLIONS: Rub the scallions with the remaining 1 tablespoon olive oil and grill for 1 to 2 minutes on each side, or until tender. Season to taste with salt and pepper.

Arrange 4 scallions in the center of each plate and top with a piece of fish. Spoon the tomato sauce over the fish and around the plate.

For a wonderful flavor variation, you can smoke the tomatoes before adding them to the sauce. To smoke the tomatoes, soak 1 cup hickory chips in water for 1 hour. Place 1 cup dry hickory chips in the base of your grill and use a propane torch or electric starter until you get a strong smoke from the chips. Add the wet chips to the grill, cut the tomatoes into quarters, and place on the grill rack. Cover and let the tomatoes smoke for $1^1/_2$ to 2 hours, or until they have a strong smoky flavor. This can be done up to 1 day ahead. Then proceed as directed for the sauce.

Sautéed Catfish with Caramelized Onion Risotto

SERVES 4

RISOTTO

2 large yellow onions, julienned

3 tablespoons unsalted butter

1 cup arborio rice

4 cups chicken stock (see page 4)

2 tablespoons, chopped fresh flat-leaf parsley

3 tablespoons grated Parmesan cheese

Salt and freshly ground black pepper

4 5-ounce catfish fillets, skinned

Salt and freshly ground black pepper

1 tablespoon canola oil

2 tablespoons chopped fresh flat-leaf parsley

$^3/_4$ cup meat stock reduction (see page 4), warmed

TO PREPARE THE RISOTTO: Cook the onions and butter in a large sauté pan over medium heat for 8 to 10 minutes, or until golden brown and caramelized. Add the rice and cook for 2 minutes, stirring frequently. Slowly add $^1/_4$ cup of the chicken stock and stir until completely absorbed. Add the remaining stock $^1/_4$ cup at a time, stirring continuously with a smooth, gentle motion until the liquid is completely absorbed. (The risotto will take 40 to 50 minutes to cook completely.) Stir in the parsley and Parmesan cheese and season to taste with salt and pepper.

TO PREPARE THE CATFISH: Season the catfish with salt and pepper and place in a hot sauté pan with the canola oil. Cook over medium-high heat for 2 to 3 minutes on each side, or until just cooked.

Spoon the risotto in the center of each plate and top with the catfish. Sprinkle the parsley over the catfish and spoon the chicken stock reduction around the plate.

> This risotto has a slight sweetness but is still fairly neutral. Any type of herbs could be substituted for the parsley for different flavor variations.

Slow-Roasted Salmon
with Garlic and Thyme Risotto

SERVES 4

1 yellow onion, peeled and chopped

1 carrot, peeled and chopped

1 celery stalk, chopped

1 cup thyme sprigs

2 tablespoons canola oil

4 5-ounce salmon fillets, skinned

Salt and freshly ground
black pepper

RISOTTO

4 shallots, chopped

1 tablespoon minced garlic

2 tablespoons unsalted butter

1 cup arborio rice

4 cups chicken stock (see page 4)

$^1/_4$ cup cloves roasted garlic
(see page 5), with the cooking oil
reserved

1 teaspoon chopped fresh
thyme sprigs

3 tablespoons grated
Parmesan cheese

Salt and freshly ground
black pepper

$^3/_4$ cup meat stock reduction
(see page 4), warm

1 teaspoon fresh thyme leaves

TO PREPARE THE SALMON: Preheat the oven to 225°. Cook the onion, carrot, celery, and 4 sprigs of the thyme in the canola oil in a medium sauté pan over medium-low heat for 10 minutes, or until the onion is translucent. Season both sides of the salmon with salt and pepper. Place the vegetables in a small roasting pan and lay the salmon on top of the vegetables. Cover the salmon with the remaining thyme sprigs and roast in the oven for 35 to 45 minutes, or until just done.

MEANWHILE, PREPARE THE RISOTTO: Cook the shallots and minced garlic in the butter in a large sauté pan over medium heat for 3 minutes, or until translucent. Add the rice and cook for 2 minutes, stirring frequently. Slowly add $^1/_4$ cup of the chicken stock and stir until completely absorbed. Add the remaining stock $^1/_4$ cup at a time, stirring continuously with a smooth, gentle motion until the liquid is completely absorbed. (The risotto will take 40 to 50 minutes to cook completely.) Stir in 3 tablespoons of the roasted garlic, the thyme, and the Parmesan cheese. Season to taste with salt and pepper.

Spoon some of the risotto in the center of each bowl and top with the salmon. Arrange the remaining 1 tablespoon of garlic cloves around the bowl. Spoon the meat stock reduction around the bowls and drizzle with some of the reserved garlic oil. Garnish with fresh thyme leaves.

> Slow roasting is a great technique for cooking salmon because its high fat content keeps it from drying out, while the slow cooking results in an incredibly moist, delicately flavored piece of fish. Salmon is the only commonly found fish that can stand up to this cooking method.

Cold-Poached Salmon with Shaved Fennel and Apple Salad

SERVES 4

POACHING BROTH

¹/₂ cup chopped yellow onion

¹/₂ cup chopped carrot

¹/₂ cup chopped celery

¹/₂ cup chopped Granny Smith apple

¹/₂ cup chopped leeks

1 tablespoon black peppercorns

2 bay leaves

2 quarts water

¹/₃ cup fresh tarragon leaves

1 1-pound salmon fillet, skinned and cut into 8 pieces

Salt and freshly ground black pepper

SALAD

¹/₄ cup freshly squeezed lemon juice

2 tablespoons chopped fresh tarragon

5 tablespoons extra virgin olive oil

5 tablespoons canola oil

Salt and freshly ground black pepper

1 Granny Smith apple, peeled, cored, and halved

1 bulb fennel, thinly sliced

TO PREPARE THE POACHING BROTH: Place the onion, carrot, celery, apple, leeks, peppercorns, bay leaves, and water in a medium saucepan and simmer over medium heat for 30 minutes. Add the tarragon and continue to cook for 2 minutes. Strain the mixture through a fine-mesh sieve, discarding the solids, and return the broth to the saucepan. Bring the broth to a simmer over medium-low heat and remove from the heat.

TO PREPARE THE SALMON: Place the salmon in a shallow pan and pour in the warm broth. Let stand for 2 minutes, turn the salmon over, and let stand for 3 to 5 minutes, or until the salmon is cooked medium. Remove the salmon from the liquid and season with salt and pepper.

TO PREPARE THE VINAIGRETTE: Whisk together the lemon juice, tarragon, and olive and canola oils in a small bowl and season to taste with salt and pepper.

TO PREPARE THE SALAD: Combine the apple and fennel in a bowl. Toss with ¹/₂ cup of the vinaigrette and season with salt and pepper.

Spoon some of the salad in the center of each plate and top with 2 pieces of the salmon. Drizzle the remaining vinaigrette over the salmon and around the plates.

> Cold poaching gently cooks the fish and keeps it very moist. Don't rush to get the rest of the dish finished once the salmon is cooked. It is best served at room temperature. In fact, once the broth has cooled a bit, the salmon can be returned to the broth and held at room temperature for up to 1 hour.

Grilled Salmon Steaks with Marinated Tomatoes and Eggplant

SERVES 4

2 tablespoons balsamic vinegar (see note, page 130)

1 tablespoon chopped fresh basil

1 small shallot, finely diced

1/2 cup extra virgin olive oil

Salt and freshly ground black pepper

3 tomatoes, cut into eighths

1 small eggplant, peeled and cut into 1/2-inch-thick slices

4 6-ounce salmon steaks

TO PREPARE THE TOMATOES: Whisk together the balsamic vinegar, basil, shallot, and 6 tablespoons of the olive oil in a medium bowl. Season to taste with salt and pepper. Add the tomatoes and toss gently until well coated. Let stand at room temperature for 30 minutes.

Prepare a medium-hot grill. Wrap the tomatoes and the liquid in aluminum foil, making sure to seal the foil tightly, and grill for 5 to 7 minutes, or until warm. Place the tomatoes in a medium bowl, reserving the liquid separately in a small bowl.

TO PREPARE THE EGGPLANT: Brush the eggplant with 1 tablespoon of the olive oil and season with salt and pepper. Grill over a medium-hot fire for 2 to 3 minutes on each side, or until tender. Dice the eggplant, toss with the tomatoes, and season to taste with salt and pepper.

TO PREPARE THE SALMON: Brush the salmon lightly with the remaining 1 tablespoon olive oil and season with salt and pepper. Grill over a medium-hot fire for 2 to 3 minutes on each side, or until cooked medium-rare to medium.

Spoon some of the tomato-eggplant mixture in the center of each plate and top with a salmon steak. Drizzle the reserved tomato liquid over the salmon and around the plates.

> This is my favorite type of dish to cook at home. It's very simple to prepare, loaded with flavor, and leaves very few dishes to wash.

Sautéed Snapper with Caramelized Onion–Strewn Grits and Red Wine Pan Sauce

SERVES 4

GRITS

1¹/₂ cups water

2 teaspoons salt

¹/₂ cup white grits

1 red onion, julienned

1 tablespoon unsalted butter

2 tablespoons chopped
fresh chives

1 tablespoon freshly squeezed
lemon juice

Salt and freshly ground
black pepper

4 5-ounce snapper fillets, skin on

Salt and freshly ground
black pepper

2 tablespoons canola oil

1 shallot, diced

1 cup red wine

¹/₂ cup extra virgin olive oil

1 tablespoon cider vinegar

1 tablespoon chopped fresh chives

TO PREPARE THE GRITS: Place the water and salt in a medium saucepan and bring to a boil. Stir in the grits, decrease the heat to low, and simmer for 25 to 30 minutes, or until the grits are soft.

Cook the red onion and butter in a small sauté pan over medium heat for 10 to 12 minutes, or until golden brown and caramelized. Fold the onion, chives, and lemon juice into the cooked grits, season to taste with salt and pepper, and keep warm.

TO PREPARE THE SNAPPER: Season the snapper with salt and pepper and score the skin side with a sharp knife or razor blade. Heat the canola oil in a large sauté pan over medium-high heat. Cook the snapper, skin side down first, for 2 minutes on each side, or until golden brown. Remove from the pan, cover, and keep warm.

TO PREPARE THE SAUCE: Cook the shallot in the same pan over medium heat for 2 to 3 minutes, or until translucent. Add the wine and cook over medium-high heat for 10 minutes, or until reduced to ¹/₄ cup. Add the olive oil, vinegar, and chives and stir well. Season with salt and pepper.

Spoon some of the grits in the center of each plate and top with a piece of snapper. Drizzle the pan sauce over the snapper and around the plate.

> Grits have a very neutral flavor, making them the perfect medium for showing off other ingredients. Here I have paired them with caramelized onion to give them a little sweetness, but you can flavor them with any herb or even with roasted peppers.

Ponzu-Marinated Scallops with Daikon and Bok Choy

SERVES 4

12 large sea scallops

3/4 cup ponzu sauce

1 tablespoon canola oil

3 tablespoons sesame oil

1 tablespoon peeled and minced fresh ginger

2 cups thinly sliced bok choy

1/2 cup julienned daikon (see note, page 31)

1 tablespoon freshly squeezed orange juice

1 teaspoon mirin (see note, page 31)

1/2 teaspoon chopped fresh cilantro

Salt and freshly ground black pepper

1/4 cup 1-inch-long fresh chive pieces

TO PREPARE THE SCALLOPS: Place the scallops and ponzu sauce in a resealable plastic bag and marinate in the refrigerator for 2 hours. Cook the marinated scallops with the canola oil in a hot sauté pan over medium-high heat for 1 to 2 minutes on each side, or until just undercooked. Remove the scallops from the pan and keep warm.

TO PREPARE THE VEGETABLES: Heat the sesame oil and ginger in a medium sauté pan over medium-high heat. Add the bok choy and daikon and cook, stirring frequently, for 2 to 3 minutes, or until the bok choy is tender. Add the orange juice, mirin, and cilantro and season to taste with salt and pepper.

Arrange some of the stir-fried vegetables in the center of each plate. Place 3 scallops on top of the vegetables and spoon the cooking liquid from the bok choy around the plate. Sprinkle with the chives.

> Ponzu is a Japanese dipping sauce made with lemon juice or rice wine vinegar, soy sauce, mirin or sake, and kombu (seaweed). It is usually used as a dipping sauce for sushi. Ponzu is available in the Asian section of many grocery stores and in Asian markets. If you are unable to find it, marinate the scallops in 1/3 cup tamari (see note, page 31), 1/4 cup mirin, and 1 tablespoon rice wine vinegar.

Grilled Scallop and
Red Onion Brochettes

SERVES 4

MARINADE

1/4 cup freshly squeezed
orange juice

2 tablespoons soy sauce

1 1/2 tablespoons chopped
fresh ginger

1 tablespoon chopped garlic

5 tablespoons extra virgin olive oil

3 tablespoons chopped lemongrass

1/2 jalapeño chile, seeded
and chopped

1/4 cup chopped fresh cilantro

1/4 cup chopped scallions

1 1/2 tablespoons freshly squeezed
lime juice

24 sea scallops

1 red onion, cut into bite-sized
wedges

2/3 cup white rice

1 1/2 cups water

1/4 cup chopped scallions

3 tablespoons unsalted butter

Salt and freshly ground
black pepper

1 teaspoon fresh amaranth

TO PREPARE THE MARINADE: Combine the orange juice, soy sauce, ginger, garlic, olive oil, lemongrass, jalapeño, cilantro, scallions, and lime juice in a small bowl.

TO PREPARE THE BROCHETTES: Alternate the scallops and onion wedges on 8 skewers. Place the skewers in a large, resealable plastic bag and pour in the marinade. Refrigerate for 2 hours.

TO PREPARE THE RICE: Combine the rice and water in a medium saucepan, cover, and simmer over medium-low heat for 20 to 25 minutes, or until tender.

Cook the scallions in the butter in a small sauté pan over medium-low heat for 5 minutes, or until the scallions are soft. Add to the rice and cook for 5 minutes, or until warm. Season to taste with salt and pepper.

TO COOK THE BROCHETTES: Prepare a medium-hot grill. Remove the brochettes from the marinade and season with salt and pepper. Grill for 3 to 4 minutes on each side, or until the scallops are just cooked.

Place some of the rice in the center of each plate and top with 1 or 2 brochettes. Top with freshly ground black pepper and garnish with fresh amaranth.

> You could use Vidalia, Maui, or Spanish onions instead of red onion in this recipe. The important thing is using an onion that will be sweet enough to eat when partially cooked. Also, consider using a fresh rosemary sprig as the skewer, if available. It adds a lovely visual touch to the brochette.

Lobster Tail with Horseradish Potatoes and Haricots Verts

SERVES 4

POTATOES

2 pounds potatoes,
peeled and quartered

1 cup milk

2 tablespoons unsalted butter

$2/3$ cup grated fresh horseradish

Salt and freshly ground
black pepper

$1/2$ cup unsalted butter

$1/3$ cup grated fresh horseradish

2 tablespoons chopped
fresh chives

4 lobster tails, boiled and shelled

2 cups haricots verts, parboiled
and cut on the diagonal

1 teaspoon lemon zest

1 teaspoon tiny green basil leaves

1 teaspoon tiny purple basil leaves

TO PREPARE THE POTATOES: Place the potatoes in a large pot of salted water and bring to a boil. Cook for 20 to 25 minutes, or until tender. Drain the water, add the milk and butter to the pot, and bring to a full boil over high heat. Remove from the heat, add the horseradish, and whip the potatoes with an electric mixer or hand masher until smooth. Season to taste with salt and pepper, cover, and keep warm until ready to use.

TO PREPARE THE LOBSTER: Heat the butter, horseradish, and the chives in a medium sauté pan over medium heat. Add the lobster and cook for 5 minutes, or until hot.

Spoon some of the potatoes in the center of each plate. Slice each lobster tail into 5 pieces. Arrange the haricots verts next to the potatoes and top with a sliced lobster tail. Spoon the butter mixture from the lobster over the plate. Sprinkle with lemon zest and garnish with tiny green and purple basil leaves.

Heating the lobster in the horseradish butter adds richness and a little bit of sharpness to the lobster, but garlic, herb, or citrus butter would also work well.

If you cannot find fresh horseradish, substitute prepared horseradish, but decrease the quantity by half.

Grilled Shrimp and Vegetables with Linguine

SERVES 4

MARINADE

3 tablespoons balsamic
vinegar (see note, page 130)

1 teaspoon finely chopped garlic

3 fresh basil leaves, finely chopped

1/2 cup extra virgin olive oil

Salt and freshly ground
black pepper

2 large zucchini, sliced lengthwise
1/2 inch thick

2 large yellow squashes, sliced
lengthwise 1/2 inch thick

1 large red onion, cut into
1/2-inch-thick slices

2 large red tomatoes, halved

16 large shrimp, peeled
and deveined

Salt and freshly ground
black pepper

8 ounces linguine

1 teaspoon tiny green basil leaves

1 teaspoon tiny purple basil leaves

1 teaspoon extra virgin olive oil

TO PREPARE THE MARINADE: Place the balsamic vinegar, garlic, and basil in a small bowl and whisk in the olive oil. Season to taste with salt and pepper and set aside.

TO PREPARE THE SHRIMP AND VEGETABLES: Prepare a medium grill. Brush the zucchini, squashes, onion, tomatoes, and shrimp with the marinade. Place the tomatoes, cut side up, on the grill away from the flame and cook for 10 minutes. Place the onion slices over the flame and cook for 3 minutes on each side. Add the zucchini, squash, and shrimp to the grill and cook for 1 to 2 minutes on each side, or until done.

Purée the tomatoes and half of the onion for 2 minutes, or until smooth. Strain the purée through a fine-mesh sieve into a small saucepan and season to taste with salt and pepper. Keep warm.

Cut the zucchini, squashes, and the remaining onion slices into bite-sized pieces, toss together in a large bowl, and season to taste with salt and pepper. Keep warm.

MEANWHILE, PREPARE THE LINGUINE: Bring a large pot of salted water to a boil. Add the linguine and cook for 7 to 10 minutes, or until al dente. Toss the linguine with the zucchini mixture.

Spoon some of the linguine and vegetables in the center of each plate. Spoon the tomato purée over the linguine and top with the shrimp. Sprinkle with the tiny green and purple basil leaves. Drizzle with extra virgin olive oil and sprinkle with freshly ground black pepper.

This is a quick, easy dish to prepare, yet it is loaded with flavor. I used zucchini and squash in this recipe, but almost any type of vegetable would work well.

Sautéed Sea Scallops
with Wild Mushroom Stew

SERVES 4

STEW

1 pound button mushrooms, cleaned

2 cloves garlic

1 cup chopped yellow onions

4 cups cold water

1 leek, julienned (white part only)

1/4 cup unsalted butter

2 cups mixed roasted wild mushrooms (see page 5), cut into large dice

Salt and freshly ground black pepper

12 large sea scallops

Salt and freshly ground black pepper

1 tablespoon canola oil

2 tablespoons chopped fresh garlic chives

2 teaspoons extra virgin olive oil

TO PREPARE THE STEW: Combine the button mushrooms, garlic, onions, and water in a large saucepan and simmer over medium-low heat for 2 hours. Strain through a fine-mesh sieve, discarding the solids.

Cook the leek in the butter in a medium saucepan over medium-low heat for 10 minutes, or until very soft. Add the mushroom broth and stir until combined. Add the roasted mushrooms and cook for 5 minutes, or until warm. Season to taste with salt and pepper.

TO PREPARE THE SCALLOPS: Season the scallops with salt and pepper and cook with the canola oil in a hot sauté pan over medium-high heat for 2 to 3 minutes on each side, or until just cooked.

Spoon some of the mushroom stew into 4 shallow bowls and top with 3 scallops. Sprinkle the garlic chives over the scallops and around the bowl and drizzle with the olive oil.

> Garlic chives are a variety of chives that are quite a bit thicker than regular chives and have a distinct garlic flavor. If they are unavailable, regular chives will work as well.

Panko-and-Horseradish-Crusted Shrimp with Miso Broth

SERVES 4

BROTH

1 tablespoon red miso

4 cups chicken stock (see page 4)

1 tablespoon tamari
(see note, page 31)

1 tablespoon mirin (see note,
page 31)

$1/2$ cup chopped scallions

SHRIMP

1 cup panko (see note, page 115)

$1/2$ cup grated fresh horseradish

16 large shrimp, peeled and
deveined, with tails left on

Salt and freshly ground
black pepper

$1/2$ cup flour

1 egg yolk whisked with
2 tablespoons water

Canola oil for frying

TO PREPARE THE MISO BROTH: Combine the miso, stock, tamari, mirin, and scallions in a medium saucepan and cook over medium heat for 10 minutes, or until hot. Keep warm.

TO PREPARE THE SHRIMP: Combine the panko and horseradish in a small bowl. Season the shrimp with salt and pepper and lightly dust with the flour, patting off any excess. Dip the shrimp in the egg yolk mixture and coat evenly with the bread crumb mixture.

Pour canola oil to a depth of 3 inches into a deep sauté pan or a saucepan and heat to 350°. Fry the shrimp for 3 to 4 minutes, or until lightly golden brown. Remove the shrimp and blot on paper towels.

Pour the warm miso broth into 4 small bowls. Place each bowl on a plate and arrange 4 shrimp around the bowl.

> Miso is a fermented soybean paste that is frequently used in Japanese cooking. It is extremely nutritious, with large amounts of vitamin B and protein. It can be found in many grocery stores or in Asian markets and health food stores.

Herb-Crusted Halibut with Roasted Potatoes and Shiitake Mushroom Sauce

SERVES 4

3 large potatoes, peeled and cut into 3/4-inch dice

3 tablespoons extra virgin olive oil

2 tablespoons chopped fresh parsley

Salt and freshly ground black pepper

1 cup roasted shiitake mushrooms (see page 5), with the cooking liquid

1 1-pound halibut fillet, skinned and cut into 8 pieces

2 tablespoons chopped fresh chives

2 tablespoons chopped fresh chervil

TO PREPARE THE POTATOES: Preheat the oven to 350°. Place the potatoes in a medium bowl with the olive oil and parsley and toss. Spread the potatoes evenly on a baking sheet, season with salt and pepper, and roast for 20 to 25 minutes, or until golden brown.

MEANWHILE, PREPARE THE SAUCE: Place the roasted mushrooms and cooking liquid in a small saucepan and cook over medium heat for 5 minutes, or until warm. Purée until smooth, adding a little water if necessary. Season to taste with salt and pepper.

TO PREPARE THE HALIBUT: Bring water to a boil in a steamer. Season both sides of the halibut with salt and pepper. Coat the top of the halibut with the chives and chervil. Place in the steamer, cover, and cook for 3 minutes, or until just done. Keep warm.

Place some of the roasted potatoes in the center of each plate and top with 2 pieces of halibut. Spoon the mushroom purée around the plate.

> Steaming fish that is crusted with herbs allows the flavors of the herbs to penetrate into the fish so well that if the herbs were removed after cooking, the fish would still retain those flavors. This is a easy way to cook low-fat, flavorful fish.

Grilled Halibut with Warm Tomato and Roasted Garlic Salad

SERVES 4

WARM SALAD

$1/2$ cup thinly sliced red onion

$1/4$ cup balsamic vinegar
(see note, page 130)

$1/4$ cup cloves roasted garlic
(see page 5), with the cooking oil

1 cup red teardrop tomatoes

1 cup yellow teardrop tomatoes

4 5-ounce halibut fillets, skinned

Salt and freshly ground
black pepper

1 tablespoon canola oil

2 tablespoons chopped
fresh chives

TO PREPARE THE WARM SALAD: Preheat the oven to 450°. Combine the onion, balsamic vinegar, garlic, and $3/4$ cup of the garlic cooking oil in a small baking pan. Toss the tomatoes in the mixture and roast for 10 minutes, or until the tomatoes begin to split.

TO PREPARE THE HALIBUT: Prepare a medium-hot grill. Season the halibut with salt and pepper and rub with the canola oil. Grill the halibut for 3 to 4 minutes on each side, or until just done.

Spoon some of the tomato mixture in the center of each plate and top with a piece of halibut. Spoon some of the remaining juices from the tomatoes on the halibut and sprinkle with the chives.

> I use teardrop tomatoes in this recipe because they are firmer and smaller than cherry tomatoes. If teardrops aren't available, substitute small cherry tomatoes, but watch the cooking time. Because they are softer, cherry tomatoes will cook a little faster.

Fettuccine and Spinach in Saffron-Mussel Broth

SERVES 4

2 pounds mussels, cleaned and debearded

5 cloves garlic

$1/8$ teaspoon saffron threads

2 tablespoons minced shallots

2 cups white wine

2 cups chicken stock (see page 4)

2 tablespoons chopped fresh chives

2 tablespoons chopped fresh flat-leaf parsley

2 cups fresh baby spinach leaves, cleaned

Salt and freshly ground black pepper

8 ounces fettuccine

TO PREPARE THE MUSSELS: Discard any mussels that have opened and do not close when gently tapped on a work surface. Place the garlic, saffron, shallots, white wine, stock, chives, and parsley in a stockpot and bring to a simmer over medium-low heat. Add the mussels, cover, and cook for 3 to 5 minutes, or until all of the mussels have opened. (If a mussel does not open after cooking, throw it away.) Remove the mussels from the pan and set aside. Add the spinach to the stockpot, and stir until wilted. Season to taste with salt and pepper.

TO PREPARE THE FETTUCCINE: While the mussels are cooking, bring a large pot of salted water to a boil. Add the fettuccine to the pan and cook for 7 to 10 minutes, or until al dente. Drain and keep warm.

Place some of the fettuccine in the center of each bowl and top with some of the mussels. Ladle the mussel broth into the bowls and top with freshly ground black pepper.

> Saffron is the yellow stigmas from a small purple crocus. Each flower produces only 3 stigmas and they must be harvested by hand, and then dried. It takes some 14,000 dried stigmas to make 1 ounce of saffron, which explains why it is the most expensive spice. Luckily, with saffron, a little goes a long way.

poultry

107 | Chicken Roulade with Blue Cheese, Black Walnuts, and Spinach and Basmati Rice

108 | Thyme-and-Mustard-Marinated Grilled Chicken with Horseradish Potato Salad

109 | Orange Blossom Honey–Glazed Chicken with Roasted Sweet Potato Purée

110 | Almond-Crusted Chicken Breast with Spinach and Citrus Vinaigrette

113 | Cumin-Garlic-Rubbed Cornish Hens with Potato-Parmesan Pavé

115 | Panko-and-Ginger-Crusted Chicken with Stir-Fried Vegetables and Sweet and Sour Mustard Sauce

116 | Tamari-and-Ginger-Roasted Turkey with Lemon-Ginger Jasmine Rice

117 | Sautéed Duck Breasts with Swiss Chard, Ginger-Braised Celery, and Orange Vinaigrette

119 | Whole Roasted Duck with Red Wine–Braised Apples

120 | Peppercorn-and-Thyme-Roasted Goose

Chicken Roulade with Blue Cheese, Black Walnuts, and Spinach and Basmati Rice

2 tablespoons chopped shallots

1/4 cup unsalted butter

8 ounces blue cheese, crumbled

1/2 cup black walnuts, toasted (see note, page 36) and chopped

1 small yellow onion, chopped

1 cup basmati rice

3 cups water

1 tablespoon chopped fresh chives

Salt and freshly ground black pepper

4 boneless, skinless chicken breasts

1 cup fresh spinach leaves, cleaned and stemmed

2 tablespoons extra virgin olive oil

Roulade is the French term for a thin piece of meat rolled around some type of filling. Black walnuts have a stronger flavor than regular walnuts, and they can stand up to the intensity of the blue cheese, but if you have trouble finding them, regular walnuts will be fine.

TO PREPARE THE FILLING: Cook the shallots in 2 tablespoons of the butter in a small sauté pan over medium heat for 4 minutes, or until lightly golden. Remove from the heat and cool to room temperature. Combine the shallots, all but 1 tablespoon of the blue cheese, and all but 1 tablespoon of the walnuts in a small bowl, mix well, and set aside.

TO PREPARE THE RICE: Cook the remaining 2 tablespoons butter and the onion in a large saucepan over medium heat for 5 minutes, or until the onion is translucent. Add the rice and stir until well coated. Add the water, cover, and cook for 20 to 25 minutes, or until the rice is tender. Fold in the chives, season to taste with salt and pepper, and keep warm.

TO PREPARE THE CHICKEN: Preheat the oven to 375°. Lay the chicken breasts flat on a cutting board and pound with a mallet until they're about 1/4 inch thick. Season both sides with salt and pepper. Layer the spinach on top of the chicken and spoon the filling along one edge of each piece. Tightly roll up the chicken breasts and tie together with kitchen string.

Heat the olive oil in a small roasting pan on the stove top over medium-high heat. Sear the chicken for 2 minutes on all sides, or until golden brown. Place the pan in the oven and roast for 20 minutes, or until done. Remove from the oven and let rest for 5 minutes. Remove the string and, using a very sharp knife, cut each roulade crosswise into 4 slices.

Spoon some of the rice in the center of each plate and top with the roulade slices. Sprinkle the remaining blue cheese and walnuts around each plate and serve immediately.

Thyme-and-Mustard-Marinated Grilled Chicken with Horseradish Potato Salad

SERVES 4

2 tablespoons extra virgin olive oil

2 tablespoons whole-grain mustard

4 boneless, skinless chicken breasts

Salt and freshly ground black pepper

4 sprigs thyme

POTATO SALAD

2 tablespoons grated fresh horseradish

2 tablespoons rice wine vinegar

2 teaspoons fresh thyme leaves

$1/2$ cup extra virgin olive oil

Salt and freshly ground black pepper

2 pounds small red potatoes

$1/2$ cup sliced celery

TO MARINATE THE CHICKEN: Combine the olive oil and mustard in a small bowl and brush on the chicken. Season the chicken with pepper and place in a resealable bag with the thyme sprigs. Refrigerate for at least 4 hours.

TO PREPARE THE POTATO SALAD: Purée the horseradish, vinegar, thyme leaves, and olive oil and season to taste with salt and pepper. Set aside.

Place the potatoes in a large pot of salted water. Bring to a boil and cook for 20 to 25 minutes, or until tender. Drain and allow the potatoes to cool slightly. Quarter each potato and toss with the celery and $1/2$ cup of the vinaigrette until well coated. Keep warm until ready to serve.

TO COOK THE CHICKEN: Prepare a medium-hot grill. Season the chicken with salt and grill for 4 to 5 minutes on each side, or until done. Slice each chicken breast on the diagonal before serving.

Layer the chicken slices, overlapping them, on one side of each plate and spoon some of the potato salad next to it. Drizzle the vinaigrette over the chicken and top with freshly ground black pepper.

> This dish could easily be served as a salad. Simply cut the chicken into bite-sized pieces, toss with the potatoes, celery, and vinaigrette, and serve warm or cold.

Orange Blossom Honey–Glazed Chicken with Roasted Sweet Potato Purée

SERVES 4

1 cup orange blossom honey

$1/4$ cup chicken stock
(see page 4)

1 3- to 4-pound chicken

Salt and freshly ground
black pepper

3 sweet potatoes

2 tablespoons unsalted butter

TO PREPARE THE GLAZE: Place the honey and stock in a small saucepan and whisk over medium heat for 5 minutes, or until smooth. Reserve $1/4$ cup of the glaze for the sweet potatoes and $1/3$ cup for the sauce.

TO PREPARE THE CHICKEN: Preheat the oven to 325°. Place the chicken in a roasting pan and season with salt and pepper. Thoroughly brush the chicken with the glaze and roast for 45 to 60 minutes, or until the juices run clear. Brush on additional glaze every 15 minutes during the roasting. Remove from the oven, let rest for 10 minutes, and carve.

MEANWHILE, PREPARE THE SWEET POTATOES: Prick the sweet potatoes with a fork and bake alongside the chicken for 45 minutes, or until soft. Remove the skins and place the sweet potatoes in a bowl with the butter and $1/4$ cup of the glaze. Using an electric mixer or hand masher, whip the potatoes until smooth.

TO PREPARE THE SAUCE: Drain the pan drippings from the chicken and remove and discard the fat. Cook the drippings and the $1/3$ cup reserved glaze in a small saucepan over medium heat for 5 minutes, or until warm.

Spoon some of the sweet potatoes on one side of each plate. Layer the chicken slices in an overlapping pattern alongside the potatoes, and spoon the sauce over the chicken.

> Orange blossom honey has a slight orange-flower flavor that is an excellent accompaniment to chicken. If you cannot find orange blossom honey, substitute clover honey. This simple dish is always a hit with kids.

Almond-Crusted Chicken Breast with Spinach and Citrus Vinaigrette

SERVES 4

VINAIGRETTE

3 tablespoons freshly squeezed orange juice

2 tablespoons freshly squeezed lemon juice

$^3/_4$ cup extra virgin olive oil

Salt and freshly ground black pepper

4 boneless chicken breasts

Salt and freshly ground black pepper

$^1/_4$ cup finely chopped almonds

2 tablespoons canola oil

6 cups fresh spinach, cleaned and stemmed

12 naval orange segments

1 teaspoon amaranth grain

1 tablespoon fresh soft baby thyme

TO PREPARE THE VINAIGRETTE: Combine the orange juice and lemon juice in a small bowl. Whisk in the olive oil and season to taste with salt and pepper.

TO PREPARE THE CHICKEN: Season the chicken breasts with salt and pepper and press the almonds on top to form a crust. Place the canola oil in a hot sauté pan, add the chicken, and cook for 3 minutes on each side, or until done.

TO PREPARE THE SPINACH: Cook the spinach and $^1/_2$ cup of the vinaigrette in a large sauté pan over medium-high heat for 2 minutes, or until the spinach is just wilted.

Place a bed of spinach in the center of each plate and top with a chicken breast. Spoon the vinaigrette over the chicken and around the plate. Top with freshly ground black pepper and garnish with fresh orange segments, amaranth grains, and baby thyme.

With just a few minor changes this combination of ingredients will make a delicious salad. Increase the almonds to $^1/_2$ cup and combine with $^1/_2$ cup bread crumbs (see note, page 20). Cut the chicken breasts in strips, dredge in the crumb mixture, and cook according to the directions. Toss the spinach with the vinaigrette, but do not cook. Place a bed of spinach on each plate and top with some of the warm chicken strips.

Cumin-Garlic-Rubbed Cornish Hens with Potato-Parmesan Pavé

SERVES 8

PAVÉ

4 large potatoes, peeled and thinly sliced

3 cups heavy cream

Salt and freshly ground black pepper

1/2 cup freshly grated Parmesan cheese

4 small Cornish game hens

2 tablespoons extra virgin olive oil

Salt and freshly ground black pepper

1/4 cup crushed cumin seeds

4 cloves garlic, minced

1 cup chicken stock (see page 4)

2 teaspoons freshly squeezed lemon juice

2 tablespoons chopped fresh chives

3 tablespoons unsalted butter

1 tablespoon canola oil

1 tablespoon fresh baby thyme leaves

1 teaspoon cumin seed

TO PREPARE THE PAVÉ: Preheat the oven to 350°. In a medium bowl, toss the potato slices with the cream until thoroughly coated. Line an 8-inch square pan with aluminum foil and generously butter the foil. Arrange 4 layers of the potatoes in the bottom of the pan and season with salt and pepper. Sprinkle half of the Parmesan cheese on the potatoes and cover with 4 layers of potato. Season with salt and pepper, sprinkle on the remaining Parmesan, and layer the remaining potatoes over the cheese. Season with salt and pepper. Cover the pavé tightly with a sheet of buttered aluminum foil, buttered side down. Place another 8-inch pan over the pavé and weight it down with a brick or other heavy, ovenproof object. Bake for 1 1/2 hours, or until the potatoes are tender. Leaving the weight on, cool the pavé to room temperature, and then refrigerate for at least 4 hours.

TO PREPARE THE HENS: Preheat the oven to 400°. Rub the Cornish hens with the olive oil and season the outside and the inner cavity with salt and pepper. Combine the cumin and garlic in a small bowl and rub the mixture over the outside of each hen. Place the hens in a roasting pan and roast in the oven for 30 to 40 minutes, or until golden brown and crispy and the juices from the thigh run clear when pierced with a knife.

Remove the hens from the pan and place the roasting pan over a burner on the stove top. Add the chicken stock to the pan and cook over medium heat for 5 to 7 minutes, or until reduced to 1/2 cup. Add the lemon juice and chives and whisk in the butter. Season to taste with salt and pepper.

continued

MEANWHILE, HEAT THE PAVÉ: Remove the weight, pan, and aluminum foil from the top of the pavé. Invert the pavé onto a baking sheet, remove the bottom piece of foil, and cut into 2-inch squares using a very sharp knife. You will need a total of 8 squares. Place 4 of the squares in a large sauté pan with the canola oil and cook over medium heat for 4 to 5 minutes, or until golden brown. Carefully turn the pavé over and cook for 4 to 5 minutes, or until golden brown and warmed through. Remove from the pan and drain on paper towels. Repeat with the remaining 4 pavé squares.

Cut each Cornish hen in half along the breast bone and place half on one side of each plate. Place a piece of the sautéed pavé alongside the hen. Spoon the sauce over the hens and around the plate. Garnish with fresh baby thyme and cumin seed.

Pavé, French for "paving stone," is used to describe layered foods that are cut in squares or rectangles. This pavé is a perfect dish to make when you have guests because it can easily be prepared a day ahead and sautéed at the last moment.

Panko-and-Ginger-Crusted Chicken with Stir-Fried Vegetables and Sweet and Sour Mustard Sauce

SERVES 4

SAUCE

1/2 cup honey

1/4 cup Chinese mustard

2 tablespoons rice wine vinegar

CHICKEN

4 boneless, skinless chicken breasts

Salt and freshly ground black pepper

2 cups panko

2 tablespoons peeled and minced fresh ginger

1 egg, lightly beaten

2 tablespoons canola oil

VEGETABLES

2 tablespoons canola oil

1 tablespoon peeled and minced fresh ginger

2 cups coarsely chopped bok choy

1/2 cup julienned leeks (white part only)

1/2 cup sliced water chestnuts

1 cup bean sprouts

TO PREPARE THE SAUCE: Combine the honey, mustard, and vinegar in a small saucepan and cook over medium heat for 5 minutes, or until warm.

TO PREPARE THE CHICKEN: Cut each chicken breast lengthwise into 4 strips and season with salt and pepper. Combine the panko and the ginger in a small bowl. Dip each chicken strip in the egg and coat with the panko mixture. Heat the canola oil in a large sauté pan over medium heat and add the chicken strips. Cook for 2 to 3 minutes on each side, or until golden brown. Remove from the pan and drain on paper towels.

MEANWHILE, PREPARE THE VEGETABLES: Heat the canola oil in a large sauté pan over medium heat. Add the ginger and cook for 30 seconds. Add the bok choy, leeks, and water chestnuts and cook, stirring, for 3 minutes. Add the bean sprouts and cook for 2 minutes, or until the vegetables are just tender.

Spoon some of the vegetables in the center of each plate. Arrange the chicken over the vegetables and drizzle the sauce over the chicken and around the plate.

> Panko are the bread crumbs used for coating fried foods in Japanese cooking. They are coarser than regular bread crumbs, and they create a wonderfully crunchy crust. Panko is available in the Asian section of many grocery stores or in Asian markets. Regular bread crumbs can be substituted, but you won't be able to achieve the same light crispiness.

Tamari-and-Ginger-Roasted Turkey with Lemon-Ginger Jasmine Rice

SERVES 8

1/2 cup plus 2 tablespoons unsalted butter

1/4 cup tamari (see note, page 31)

4 tablespoons peeled and minced fresh ginger

1 10-pound turkey

Salt and freshly ground black pepper

2 small shallots, diced

1 1/4 cups jasmine rice

4 cups water

2 teaspoons minced lemon zest

TO PREPARE THE GLAZE: Preheat the oven to 375°. Melt the 1/2 cup butter in a small saucepan over medium-low heat. Remove from the heat, add the tamari and 2 tablespoons of the ginger and stir until combined.

TO PREPARE THE TURKEY: Season the outside and the cavity of the turkey with salt and pepper.

Brush the turkey with the glaze and roast for 2 1/2 to 3 hours, or until done, basting occasionally with the glaze. (You may need to cover the turkey with aluminum foil toward the end of cooking to prevent overbrowning.) Remove the turkey from the oven, let it rest for 15 minutes, and then carve.

TO PREPARE THE RICE: When the turkey is nearly finished roasting, cook the shallots and the remaining 2 tablespoons ginger with the 2 tablespoons butter in a large saucepan over medium heat for 5 minutes, or until the shallots are translucent. Add the rice and stir until well coated. Add the water, cover, and cook over medium-low heat for 20 to 25 minutes, or until the rice is tender. Fold in the lemon zest and keep warm.

TO PREPARE THE SAUCE: Drain the pan drippings from the turkey and remove the fat. Cook the drippings and any remaining glaze in a small saucepan over medium heat for 5 minutes, or until warm.

Place some of the rice on one side of each plate and layer the turkey slices in an overlapping pattern alongside the rice. Drizzle the sauce over the turkey and rice.

Either jasmine or basmati rice would work well in this dish.

Sautéed Duck Breasts with Swiss Chard, Ginger-Braised Celery, and Orange Vinaigrette

SERVES 4

VINAIGRETTE

3 tablespoons freshly squeezed orange juice

1 teaspoon freshly squeezed lemon juice

1/4 cup olive oil

1 scallion, finely chopped

1 small orange, peeled, segmented, and membranes removed

Salt and freshly ground black pepper

2 tablespoons unsalted butter

1 1-inch piece fresh ginger, peeled

4 large stalks celery, cut into 1-inch pieces on the diagonal

1 cup chicken stock (see page 4)

2 tablespoons preserved ginger (see page 6)

Salt and freshly ground black pepper

4 small duck breasts, trimmed and skin scored

3 cups chopped Swiss chard

TO PREPARE THE VINAIGRETTE: Place the orange and lemon juices in a small bowl and whisk in the olive oil. Add the scallions and orange segments, stir until combined, season to taste with salt and pepper, and set aside.

TO PREPARE THE CELERY: Place the butter, fresh ginger, celery, and 3/4 cup of the stock in a medium saucepan and cook over medium-low heat for 5 to 6 minutes, or until the celery is tender. Remove the piece of ginger and stir in the preserved ginger. Season to taste with salt and pepper and keep warm.

TO PREPARE THE DUCK: Season the duck breasts with salt and pepper and place in a very hot sauté pan over high heat with the skin side down first. Cook for 3 to 4 minutes on each side, or until the skin is golden brown and crispy and the duck is cooked medium. Remove the duck from the pan, drain the fat from the pan, and allow the duck to rest for 2 minutes.

Meanwhile, place the Swiss chard in the pan used for the duck and quickly wilt over medium-high heat with the remaining 1/4 cup stock. Season to taste with salt and pepper.

Slice the duck breasts on the diagonal. Place some Swiss chard on the center of each plate and top with some of the celery pieces. Arrange the duck breast slices on top of the celery and spoon the vinaigrette over the duck and around the plates. Top with freshly ground black pepper.

Preserved ginger adds sweetness and a little zip to any dish. I included a recipe for preserved ginger, but if you are in a rush, it can be purchased at the supermarket. There generally are two types of ginger available in jars—preserved and candied. The preserved ginger available at the supermarket is usually pickled. To get the sweetness needed for this recipe, purchase the candied ginger instead.

Whole Roasted Duck with
Red Wine–Braised Apples

SERVES 4

1 750-ml bottle red wine

2 cups honey

1 4- to 5-pound duck,
excess fat trimmed

Salt and freshly ground
black pepper

1 large yellow onion, quartered

2 carrots, peeled and chopped

2 stalks celery, chopped

3 Granny Smith apples,
peeled, cored, and cut into
$\frac{1}{2}$-inch-thick rings

2 tablespoons fresh rosemary

> If you have difficulty find-
> ing a whole duck, substitute
> breasts. Sear them, skin side
> down first, in a hot pan and
> brush often with the glaze
> during the remaining cook-
> ing time.

TO PREPARE THE GLAZE: Cook the wine in a medium sauce-pan over medium heat for 30 minutes, or until reduced to 2 cups. Stir in the honey and cook for 30 minutes, or until reduced to 3 cups. Reserve 2 cups of the glaze for the apples.

TO PREPARE THE DUCK: Preheat the oven to 400°. Season the duck cavity with salt and pepper. Pierce the skin with a fork 10 to 15 times, to release the fat during cooking. Place the onion, carrots, and celery in a roasting pan and place the duck on top. Roast for 15 minutes. Remove the duck from the oven and brush the outside with the glaze. Decrease the oven temperature to 350° and cook, basting occasionally with the glaze, for 45 to 60 minutes, or until golden brown and crispy and the juices from the cavity run clear. Remove from the oven, let rest for 15 minutes, and then carve.

MEANWHILE, PREPARE THE APPLES: About 45 minutes before the duck is ready, place the apples in a small baking pan. Pour in 2 cups of the glaze, cover, and bake at 350° for 30 minutes. Uncover and cook for 15 minutes, or until tender.

TO PREPARE THE SAUCE: Drain the cooking liquid from the apples into a small saucepan. Strain any pan drippings from the duck through a fine-mesh sieve, remove the fat, and add to the saucepan. Cook the sauce over medium heat for 5 minutes, or until warm.

Arrange apple rings in the center of each plate, sprinkle with fresh rosemary, and place sliced duck meat on top. Spoon the sauce over the duck and around each plate.

Peppercorn-and-Thyme-Roasted Goose

SERVES 4

3 tablespoons cracked mixed black, white, and green peppercorns

2 tablespoons fresh thyme leaves

$1/2$ cup extra virgin olive oil

1 tablespoon chopped garlic

Salt

1 whole goose (7 to 10 pounds), cleaned

Freshly ground black pepper

1 large yellow onion, quartered

2 carrots, peeled and chopped

2 stalks celery, chopped

$1/4$ cup unsalted butter, cut into pieces

1 tablespoon chopped fresh thyme

TO PREPARE THE GLAZE: Stir together the cracked peppercorns, thyme leaves, olive oil, and garlic in a small bowl and season with salt.

TO PREPARE THE GOOSE: Preheat the oven to 375°. Season the outside and the cavity of the goose with salt and pepper. Brush the glaze all over the outside of the goose, reserving any extra to use for basting. Place the onion, carrots, and celery in a roasting pan, and place the goose on top of the vegetables. Roast for 2 to $2^1/2$ hours, basting occasionally with the remaining glaze and any drippings, until golden brown and crispy and the juice from the cavity runs clear. Remove the goose from the oven and let rest for 15 minutes before carving.

TO PREPARE THE SAUCE: Strain the pan drippings through a fine-mesh sieve, remove the fat, and place the juices in a small saucepan over medium heat. Whisk the butter into the meat juices, add the chopped thyme, and season to taste with salt and pepper.

Carve the goose and serve with the pan sauce.

> Goose is a nice alternative to turkey. It is all dark meat with rich, buttery flesh and is fattier than turkey. This goose would go well with all of your traditional holiday dishes. If you can't find goose, you may use duck or chicken instead.

meat

123 | Red Wine–Braised Short Ribs with Garlic Mashed Potatoes

126 | Grilled Bacon-Wrapped Beef Tenderloin with
Wild Mushroom Risotto

128 | Cardamom Beef Stew with Potatoes, Celery Root, and
Parsnips

129 | Grilled Strip Loin Steaks with Rosemary-Potato Purée
and Meat Jus

130 | Grilled Beef Tenderloin with Asparagus and Roasted Red
Onion Vinaigrette

132 | Stuffed Beef Tenderloin with Whole Wheat Couscous
and Black Olive Vinaigrette

134 | Poached Beef Tenderloin with Fingerling Potatoes,
Brussels Sprouts, and Beef Broth

135 | Sautéed Veal Chops with Braised Juniper Berry–Infused
Red Cabbage

136 | Ginger-Braised Spareribs with Cilantro-Scented Navy Beans

137 | Herb-Crusted Pork Tenderloin with Roasted Yukon Gold
Potatoes and Bacon-Sherry Vinaigrette

138 | Sautéed Pork Chops with Ratatouille

140 | Whole Roasted Vidalia Onions Stuffed with Braised
      Lamb Shank and Roasted Parsnips

142 | Rack of Lamb with Crispy Polenta and Mustard Sauce

145 | Peppered Lamb Loin with Mustard Spaetzle and
      Thyme Reduction

147 | Yukon Gold Potato and Braised Oxtail Tarts

Red Wine–Braised Short Ribs
with Garlic Mashed Potatoes

SERVES 4

SHORT RIBS

1 cup chopped yellow onions

1/2 cup chopped leeks
(white part only)

6 cloves garlic, chopped

4 tablespoons canola oil

1 750-ml bottle red wine

1 teaspoon coriander seeds

8 short ribs, trimmed of excess fat

3 tablespoons extra virgin olive oil

4 sprigs thyme

Salt and freshly ground
black pepper

4 cups chicken stock (see page 4)

POTATOES

2 pounds potatoes,
peeled and quartered

1/2 cup milk

2 tablespoons unsalted butter

6 cloves roasted garlic
(see page 5)

Salt and freshly ground
black pepper

TO PREPARE THE SHORT RIBS: Cook the onions, leeks, garlic, and 2 tablespoons of the canola oil in a roasting pan on the stovetop over medium-high heat for 7 to 10 minutes, or until golden brown. Add the red wine and bring to a simmer. Remove the pan from the heat and cool to room temperature. Place the coriander seeds in a small piece of cheesecloth and tie with kitchen string to form a sachet. Add the sachet, short ribs, olive oil, and thyme to the pan, cover with plastic wrap, and refrigerate for 24 to 36 hours.

Preheat the oven to 300°. Remove the ribs from the marinade, reserving the marinade, and season with salt and pepper. Sear the ribs in a hot roasting pan with the remaining 2 tablespoons canola oil for 2 to 3 minutes on each side, or until golden brown. Add the marinade and stock, cover with aluminum foil, and braise for 3 to 4 hours, or until the meat is fork-tender.

Remove the ribs from the roasting pan, strain the braising liquid, and set aside. Just prior to serving, reheat the ribs on a baking sheet at 350° for 10 minutes, or until warm.

continued

Braising is the best method for cooking less tender cuts of meat. The key to braising meats is to cook them low and slow; the lower the temperature and the longer the cooking time, the more tender they will be. If you have the time, cooking them at 200° for 10 to 12 hours will result in meat that is so tender it will melt in your mouth.

TO PREPARE THE SAUCE: Simmer the reserved braising liquid in a medium saucepan over medium-low heat for 45 to 60 minutes, or until reduced to $1^1/_2$ cups. Keep warm.

MEANWHILE, PREPARE THE POTATOES: Place the potatoes in a large pot of salted water and bring to a boil. Cook for 20 to 25 minutes, or until tender. Drain the water, add the milk and butter to the pot, and bring to a full boil over high heat. Remove from the heat. Squeeze the roasted garlic cloves from their skins and add to the potatoes. Whip the potatoes with an electric mixer or hand masher until smooth, and season to taste with salt and pepper.

Spoon some of the potatoes slightly off center on each plate. Lean the ribs against one edge of the potatoes, and spoon the sauce over the ribs and potatoes and around the plates.

Grilled Bacon-Wrapped Beef Tenderloin with Wild Mushroom Risotto

SERVES 4

8 thick slices bacon

4 6-ounce beef tenderloin fillets

Salt and freshly ground
black pepper

RISOTTO

2 pounds button
mushrooms, cleaned

3 cloves garlic

$2^1/_2$ cups chopped yellow onions

3 quarts cold water

2 tablespoons unsalted butter

1 cup arborio rice

$1^1/_2$ cups mixed roasted wild
mushrooms (see page 5), with
the cooking liquid reserved

$1/_4$ cup freshly grated
Parmesan cheese

2 tablespoons chopped
fresh chives

Salt and freshly ground
black pepper

TO PREPARE THE BEEF: Wrap 2 slices of bacon around the outside of each fillet and tie with kitchen string. Season the fillets with salt and pepper and refrigerate until ready to use.

TO PREPARE THE MUSHROOM STOCK FOR THE RISOTTO: Combine the button mushrooms, garlic, 2 cups of the onions, and the water in a large stock pot. Simmer over medium-low heat for 2 hours and strain through a fine-mesh sieve, discarding the solids.

TO PREPARE THE RISOTTO: Cook the remaining $1/_2$ cup onion and the butter in a large sauté pan over medium heat for 3 minutes, or until translucent. Add the rice and cook for 2 minutes, stirring frequently. Slowly add $1/_4$ cup of the mushroom stock and stir until it is completely absorbed. Add the remaining mushroom stock $1/_4$ cup at a time, stirring continuously with a smooth, gentle motion, until the liquid is completely absorbed, reserving $1/_2$ cup for drizzling the beef. (The risotto will take 40 to 50 minutes to cook completely.) Cut the roasted mushrooms into bite-sized pieces and stir into the risotto. Cook for 5 minutes, or until the mushrooms are warm. Stir in the Parmesan cheese and chives and season to taste with salt and pepper.

TO COOK THE BEEF: Prepare a medium-hot grill. Grill the steaks over a medium flame for 4 minutes on each side, or until medium-rare or cooked to the desired doneness. Remove the string before serving.

Spoon some of the risotto in the center of each plate, top with a fillet, and drizzle the reserved mushroom stock over the meat and around the risotto.

Partially cooking the risotto earlier in the day will substantially reduce the time away from your guests. Cook the risotto according to the instructions, but use only three-quarters of the mushroom stock. Refrigerate it in the pan, then, just prior to serving, return the pan to the heat. Add the remaining mushroom stock in $1/4$ cup additions and continue with the recipe as directed.

Cardamom Beef Stew with Potatoes, Celery Root, and Parsnips

SERVES 4

1 cup chopped celery

1 cup chopped carrots

2 cups chopped yellow onions

2 tablespoons canola oil

20 cardamom pods, crushed

1 pound stew meat, cubed

Salt and freshly ground black pepper

1 bulb garlic, halved

6 cups meat stock (see page 3)

2 cups large-diced potatoes

1 cup large-diced celery root

1 cup large-diced parsnips

2 tablespoons extra virgin olive oil

TO PREPARE THE STEW: Preheat the oven to 350°. Place the celery, carrots, and onions in a hot roasting pan with the canola oil and cook, stirring occasionally, for 10 minutes, or until caramelized. Place the cardamom in a small piece of cheesecloth and tie with kitchen string to form a sachet. Season the beef with salt and pepper and add it to the pan along with the garlic, cardamom sachet, and stock. Cover the pan with aluminum foil and braise for 2 to 3 hours, or until the beef is very tender. Season to taste with salt and pepper.

TO PREPARE THE VEGETABLES: About 45 minutes before the beef is ready, toss the potatoes, celery root, and parsnips with the olive oil in a large bowl and spread the vegetables evenly on a baking sheet. Season with salt and pepper and roast in the oven for 45 minutes, or until golden brown.

Place some of the roasted vegetables in the center of each bowl, spoon in the stew, and top with freshly ground black pepper.

> Cardamom is a member of the ginger family and is a staple in Indian and Middle Eastern cuisine. It is available in pods or ground. I call for pods, but if they are unavailable, 1 teaspoon of ground cardamom can be substituted with similar results.

Grilled Strip Loin Steaks with Rosemary-Potato Purée and Meat Jus

SERVES 4

4 6-ounce strip steaks

¼ cup extra virgin olive oil

Freshly ground black pepper

2 tablespoons fresh
rosemary leaves

POTATO PURÉE

2 tablespoons fresh
rosemary leaves

2 pounds potatoes,
peeled and quartered

Salt

¼ cup unsalted butter

¾ cup heavy cream

Freshly ground black pepper

1 cup meat stock reduction
(see page 4), warmed

TO MARINATE THE STEAKS: Rub the steaks with the olive oil and season with pepper. Sprinkle the rosemary leaves over the steaks and refrigerate for 1 hour.

TO PREPARE THE POTATOES: Place the rosemary leaves in a small piece of cheesecloth and tie with kitchen string to form a sachet. Place the potatoes in a large pot of salted water and bring to a boil. Cook for 15 minutes, add the sachet, and cook for 10 minutes, or until the potatoes are tender. Remove the sachet and drain the potatoes. Add the butter and cream to the potatoes and cook over high heat until the cream comes to a full boil. Remove from the heat and whip with an electric mixer or hand masher until smooth. Season with salt and pepper, cover, and keep warm.

TO COOK THE STEAKS: Prepare a medium-hot grill. Season the steaks with salt and grill for 4 minutes on each side, or until medium-rare or cooked to desired doneness.

Spoon some of the potatoes in the center of each plate. Place the steak over one edge of the potatoes, and spoon the meat stock reduction over the steak and potatoes and around the plate.

This is a classic meat-and-potatoes dish with a little twist. The rosemary adds another flavor dimension, and the reduction sauce helps to tie the whole dish together. This recipe can be made with any type of steak, pork chops, pork loin, or even chicken, but if you choose chicken, use a chicken stock reduction instead of meat stock.

Grilled Beef Tenderloin with Asparagus and Roasted Red Onion Vinaigrette

SERVES 4

VINAIGRETTE

1 small red onion

3/4 cup extra virgin olive oil

3 tablespoons balsamic vinegar

2 tablespoons chopped
fresh chives

Salt and freshly ground
black pepper

1 1/2 pounds beef tenderloin

2 tablespoons extra virgin olive oil

Salt and freshly ground
black pepper

1 pound asparagus spears, trimmed

1 teaspoon red amaranth sprouts

TO PREPARE THE VINAIGRETTE: Preheat the oven to 350°. Place the onion and olive oil in a small ovenproof pan and cover tightly. Roast for 50 to 60 minutes, or until the onion is soft. Let the onion cool in the olive oil, and then remove the onion, reserving the oil. Julienne the onion and place in a medium bowl. Add the balsamic vinegar and slowly whisk in the reserved olive oil. Add the chives and season to taste with salt and pepper.

TO PREPARE THE BEEF: Prepare a medium-hot grill. Rub the beef with the olive oil and season to taste with salt and pepper. Grill for 4 to 5 minutes on each side, or until medium-rare or cooked to the desired doneness. Remove the beef from the grill, let rest for 5 minutes, and cut into 1/4-inch-thick slices.

TO PREPARE THE ASPARAGUS: Bring a medium pot of salted water to a boil. Add the asparagus and cook for 5 minutes, or until tender.

Fan the asparagus on each plate, with the stem ends in the center. Layer the beef slices in an overlapping pattern over the stem ends of the asparagus and spoon the vinaigrette over the asparagus and beef. Garnish with amaranth sprouts.

Balsamic vinegars are aged for varying lengths of time, and their virtues increase with age. Some balsamic vinegars are aged for as long as 100 years. The longer it is aged, the smoother and more syrupy the vinegar will be. Most grocery stores carry 5- and 12-year-old balsamic vinegars, with the older varieties usually sold in gourmet food stores. It is worth the money to buy, at minimum, the 12-year-old variety. It will make an enormous difference in the final flavor of any dish.

Stuffed Beef Tenderloin with Whole Wheat Couscous and Black Olive Vinaigrette

SERVES 4

VINAIGRETTE

1/2 cup chopped kalamata olives, plus 1/4 cup of their brine

1/4 cup balsamic vinegar (see note, page 130)

3/4 cup extra virgin olive oil

Salt and freshly ground black pepper

STUFFING

1 small eggplant

1 tablespoon canola oil

1 roasted poblano chile, diced (see page 5)

1 roasted red bell pepper, diced (see page 5)

6 anchovy fillets, chopped

2 12-ounce beef tenderloins

Salt and freshly ground black pepper

5 tablespoons extra virgin olive oil

3 cups water

1 tablespoon salt

1 cup whole wheat couscous

1 large red onion, julienned

2 tablespoons chopped fresh flat-leaf parsley

TO PREPARE THE VINAIGRETTE: Whisk together the olive brine and balsamic vinegar in a small bowl and then slowly whisk in the olive oil and olives. Season to taste with salt and pepper and set aside.

TO PREPARE THE STUFFING: Prepare a medium-hot grill. Peel the eggplant and cut into 1/4-inch-thick slices. Rub with the canola oil and grill for 2 minutes on each side, or until done. Dice the eggplant, place in a small bowl, and toss with the poblano, red bell pepper, and anchovies.

TO PREPARE THE BEEF: Starting from the end of each tenderloin, cut a slit all the way through the center of the tenderloin with a long, thin knife. Rotate the knife 90° and insert it into the same spot, creating an X. If the knife is not long enough to reach the far end of the loin, repeat the process starting from the other end. Insert the handle of a wooden spoon through the incision to help stretch the hole. Using your fingers and the handle of a wooden spoon to keep the incision open, stuff as much filling as possible into each tenderloin. Season the tenderloins with salt and pepper and rub with 2 tablespoons of the olive oil.

TO PREPARE THE COUSCOUS: Place the water and salt in a medium saucepan and bring to a boil. Add the couscous and bring back to a boil. Cover, remove from the heat, and let stand for 15 to 20 minutes, or until all the liquid is absorbed. Cook the red onion and 2 tablespoons of the olive oil in a medium saucepan over medium heat for 10 minutes, or until caramelized. Stir in the couscous, parsley, and remaining 1 tablespoon olive oil and cook for 10 minutes, or until warm. Season to taste with salt and pepper and keep warm.

TO COOK THE BEEF: Grill the tenderloin for 3 to 4 minutes on each side, or until medium-rare. Let rest for 5 minutes, cut into $1/4$-inch-thick slices, and season to taste with salt and pepper.

Spoon some of the couscous in the center of each plate and top with some of the beef slices. Spoon the vinaigrette over the beef and around the plates and top with freshly ground black pepper.

Stuffing a tenderloin in this manner makes an impressive presentation for your guests, but if it poses a problem, the filling can be warmed and simply spooned over the sliced meat.

Poached Beef Tenderloin with Fingerling Potatoes, Brussels Sprouts, and Beef Broth

SERVES 4

1 pound fingerling potatoes or other small white potatoes

2 cups brussels sprouts

Salt and freshly ground black pepper

6 cups meat stock (see page 3)

1¹/₂ pounds beef tenderloin, cut into 4 equal pieces

VINAIGRETTE

1¹/₂ tablespoons freshly squeezed lemon juice

1¹/₂ tablespoons minced shallots

2 tablespoons chopped fresh flat-leaf parsley

¹/₃ cup extra virgin olive oil

Salt and freshly ground black pepper

TO PREPARE THE POTATOES: Place the potatoes in a medium pot of salted water and bring to a boil. Cook for 20 to 25 minutes, or until tender. Drain and keep warm.

TO PREPARE THE BRUSSELS SPROUTS: Bring a medium pot of salted water to a boil. Add the brussels sprouts and cook for 10 minutes, or until tender. Drain, cut in half lengthwise, and season to taste with salt and pepper. Keep warm.

TO PREPARE THE BEEF: Bring the stock to a boil in a large saucepan. Place the tenderloin pieces in the stock and simmer for 7 minutes, or until the beef is cooked medium-rare. Remove the beef, let rest for 2 minutes, cut each piece into 4 slices, and season to taste with salt and pepper. Reserve the poaching liquid.

MEANWHILE, PREPARE THE VINAIGRETTE: While the beef is cooking, whisk together the lemon juice, shallots, parsley, and olive oil in a small bowl and season to taste with salt and pepper.

Arrange the potatoes and brussels sprouts in the center of each shallow bowl. Place 4 slices of the beef on the vegetables, spoon in some of the poaching liquid, and drizzle the vinaigrette over the beef.

> Poaching beef may seem odd, but it is actually a wonderful method for cooking beef tenderloin, which is very lean and can easily become dry during cooking. Poaching ensures the meat will be moist and tender.

Sautéed Veal Chops with Braised Juniper Berry–Infused Red Cabbage

SERVES 4

10 juniper berries

¼ cup unsalted butter

1 head red cabbage, thinly sliced

2 cups red wine

2 tablespoons rice wine vinegar

¼ cup sugar

Salt and freshly ground
black pepper

1 tablespoon chopped
fresh flat-leaf parsley

⅓ cup extra virgin olive oil

4 6-ounce veal loin chops

2 tablespoons canola oil

TO PREPARE THE CABBAGE: Place the juniper berries in a small piece of cheesecloth and tie with kitchen string to from a sachet. Place the butter and cabbage in a large sauté pan and cook over medium heat for 5 minutes. Add the wine, vinegar, sugar, and the sachet and simmer over medium-low heat for 15 to 20 minutes, or until the cabbage is tender. Remove the cabbage from the pan, discarding the sachet and reserving the cooking liquid, and season the cabbage to taste with salt and pepper. Add the parsley to the reserved liquid, whisk in the olive oil, and season to taste with salt and pepper.

TO PREPARE THE VEAL: Season both sides of the veal chops with salt and pepper and place in a very hot sauté pan with the canola oil. Sauté the chops over medium-high heat for 4 to 5 minutes on each side, or until cooked to the desired doneness.

Spoon some of the cabbage in the center of each plate and top with a veal chop. Spoon the reserved cooking liquid over the chop and around the plate.

> Juniper berries have a distinctive flavor that is similar to allspice without the clove—a flavor that cannot be achieved using other spices. They are sometimes sold in grocery stores in the spices section and can occasionally be found in specialty coffee and tea shops that sell spices. If you are unable to find the juniper berries, use 1 teaspoon caraway seeds instead. Using caraway will result in a completely different flavor, but it will still go well with the veal.

Ginger-Braised Spareribs with Cilantro-Scented Navy Beans

SERVES 6

1 cup chopped yellow onions

$^1/_2$ cup chopped celery

$^1/_2$ cup chopped carrot

2 tablespoons canola oil

$^1/_2$ cup chopped leeks

1 red bell pepper, seeded, deribbed, and chopped

$^1/_3$ cup peeled and sliced fresh ginger

$^1/_4$ cup dark molasses (see note, page 199)

$^1/_2$ cup brown sugar

2 tablespoons black peppercorns

3 dried chipotle chiles

5 pounds spareribs

Salt and freshly ground black pepper

6 to 8 cups meat stock (see page 3)

NAVY BEANS

2 cups navy beans, soaked overnight in water (see note, page 69)

3 cloves garlic

4 cups chicken stock (see page 4)

9 sprigs cilantro plus 4 teaspoons chopped fresh cilantro

Salt and freshly ground black pepper

TO PREPARE THE RIBS: Preheat the oven to 300°. Place a large roasting pan on the stovetop and cook the onions, celery, and carrot in the oil over medium-high heat for 10 minutes, or until caramelized. Add the leeks, bell pepper, and ginger and cook for 5 minutes. Add the molasses, sugar, peppercorns, and chiles and stir until combined. Season the ribs with salt and pepper and place on top of the vegetables. Add enough of the stock to cover the ribs and cover the pan with aluminum foil. Braise for $2^1/_2$ to 3 hours, or until the meat falls off the bone.

MEANWHILE, PREPARE THE BEANS: Drain the beans and place in a saucepan with the garlic and stock. Simmer over medium-low heat for $1^1/_2$ hours, adding water if necessary. Add the cilantro sprigs and cook for 30 minutes, or until the beans are tender. Remove the cilantro and garlic and discard. Season with salt and pepper.

TO PREPARE THE SAUCE: Remove the ribs from the liquid and strain the liquid through a fine-mesh sieve. Remove the meat from the bones, shred into small pieces, place in a saucepan, and season with salt and pepper. Cook the reserved liquid in a saucepan over medium heat for 45 minutes, or until reduced to about 3 cups. Add $^1/_4$ cup of the reduced liquid to the meat and cook over medium-low heat for 5 minutes, or until warm.

Spoon some of the beans in the center of each plate and top with the shredded meat. Spoon the sauce over the meat and beans and around the plate and sprinkle with the chopped cilantro.

> Any type of ribs would work well in this hearty dish.

Herb-Crusted Pork Tenderloin with Roasted Yukon Gold Potatoes and Bacon-Sherry Vinaigrette

SERVES 4

VINAIGRETTE

4 ounces bacon, julienned

1/2 cup olive oil

1/4 cup sherry wine vinegar

1 small shallot, finely diced

Salt and freshly ground
black pepper

1 1/2 pounds pork tenderloin

6 tablespoons extra virgin olive oil

Salt and freshly ground
black pepper

1/4 cup chopped fresh thyme

1/4 cup chopped fresh rosemary

1/2 cup chopped fresh
flat-leaf parsley

2 tablespoons canola oil

2 pounds small Yukon Gold
potatoes, quartered

TO PREPARE THE VINAIGRETTE: Cook the bacon in a small sauté pan over medium heat for 8 to 10 minutes, or until crispy. Place the bacon and 1/4 cup of the rendered bacon fat in a small bowl. Whisk in the olive oil, vinegar, and shallot and season to taste with salt and pepper.

TO PREPARE THE PORK: Preheat the oven to 375°. Rub the pork with 3 tablespoons of the olive oil and season with salt and pepper. Coat the pork with the thyme, rosemary, and 1/4 cup of the parsley. Place in a hot sauté pan with the canola oil and sear for 5 minutes on each side. Roast in the oven for 25 to 30 minutes, or until the internal temperature reaches 155° on a meat thermometer.

MEANWHILE, PREPARE THE POTATOES: Place the potatoes on a baking sheet and toss with the remaining 3 tablespoons olive oil. Sprinkle the remaining 1/4 cup parsley over the potatoes, season with salt and pepper, and roast alongside the tenderloin for 20 minutes, or until tender.

Remove the tenderloin from the oven, let it rest for 10 minutes, and then cut the meat into 1/4-inch-thick slices. Spoon some of the potatoes on one side of each plate and layer the pork slices in an overlapping pattern next to the potatoes. Drizzle the vinaigrette over the meat and potatoes and top with freshly ground pepper.

> The mild flavor of pork pairs well with herbs. I have used a combination of them here, but you could use a single herb, or add cumin, fennel seeds, or even cayenne.

Sautéed Pork Chops
with Ratatouille

SERVES 4

RATATOUILLE

$1/2$ cup diced yellow onion

4 cloves garlic, chopped

2 tablespoons extra virgin olive oil

2 cups diced eggplant

2 cups diced zucchini

2 cups diced yellow squash

2 cups diced red tomatoes

Salt and freshly ground
black pepper

4 6-ounce pork loin chops

Salt and freshly ground
black pepper

2 tablespoons canola oil

2 tablespoons fresh
chopped parsley

1 teaspoon coarse sea salt

TO PREPARE THE RATATOUILLE: Cook the onion and garlic with the olive oil in a large sauté pan over medium heat for 10 minutes, or until the onion is translucent. Add the eggplant, zucchini, and yellow squash and cook for 15 minutes, stirring frequently. Add the tomatoes and season to taste with salt and pepper. Cook for 10 minutes, or until the vegetables are tender.

TO PREPARE THE PORK: Season both sides of the pork chops with salt and pepper and place in a very hot sauté pan with the canola oil. Sauté the chops for 5 to 7 minutes on each side, or until done.

Spoon some of the ratatouille onto each plate and top with a pork chop. Spoon any juices from the ratatouille around the plate. Garnish with fresh chopped parsley and a sprinkling of coarse sea salt.

> For an interesting flavor twist, try grilling everything instead of sautéing. Finely chop the garlic and mix it with the olive oil. Cut the vegetables into $1/2$-inch-thick slices and rub them with the oil mixture. Grill the vegetables and pork chops over a medium-hot grill, and then dice the vegetables and toss them together in a large bowl. Continue with the recipe, as directed, for serving.

Whole Roasted Vidalia Onions Stuffed with Braised Lamb Shank and Roasted Parsnips

SERVES 4

2 lamb shanks

Salt and freshly ground black pepper

2 tablespoons extra virgin olive oil

1 yellow onion, chopped

1 carrot, peeled and chopped

1 stalk celery, chopped

1 cup red wine

4 cups meat stock (see page 3)

4 Vidalia or other sweet onions (see note, page 51), peeled

$1^1/_2$ cups diced parsnips

TO BRAISE THE LAMB: Preheat the oven to 300°. Season the lamb shanks with salt and pepper and cook with 1 tablespoon of the olive oil in a small roasting pan on the stove top over medium-high heat for 8 to 10 minutes, or until browned on all sides. Remove the lamb shanks, add the onion, carrot, and celery, and cook over medium-high heat for 8 to 10 minutes, or until golden brown and caramelized. Add the lamb shanks, red wine, and stock to the pan, cover tightly, and braise for 3 to 4 hours, or until the lamb is fork-tender. Remove the lamb and strip the meat from the bones into small pieces. Strain the braising liquid through a fine-mesh sieve and reserve.

MEANWHILE, PREPARE THE ONIONS: While the lamb is cooking, place the onions in a roasting pan, cover halfway with water, and bake in the oven with the lamb for $1^1/_2$ hours. Turn the onions over and bake for another $1^1/_2$ hours, or until the onions are very tender.

TO PREPARE THE PARSNIPS: About 1 hour before the lamb is ready, toss the parsnips in the remaining 1 tablespoon olive oil in a baking dish and season with salt and pepper. Roast for 1 hour, or until tender.

TO PREPARE THE SAUCE: Cook the reserved braising liquid from the lamb in a small saucepan over medium heat for 25 to 30 minutes, or until reduced to 1 cup. Season with salt and pepper. Keep warm.

TO PREPARE THE STUFFED ONIONS: Turn the oven up to 350°. Gently remove the inner layers of the onion, leaving the 3 outer layers intact. Reserve the inner layers. Combine the parsnips and lamb in a small bowl and season to taste with salt and pepper. Place the onions on a baking sheet and spoon the lamb mixture into the hollowed centers. Bake for 7 to 10 minutes, or until hot. Carefully peel off and discard the outer layer of each onion.

Purée the reserved inner layers of the onion until smooth and season to taste with salt and pepper.

Place an onion in the center of each plate, and spoon the warm sauce over the onion and around the plate. Then spoon the onion purée around the plate.

Whole roasted onions are a simple way to impress your guests. They look great on the plate and are interesting vessels for any type of grain or vegetables. Best of all, they can be prepared earlier in the day and then stuffed and heated just prior to serving.

Rack of Lamb with Crispy Polenta and Mustard Sauce

SERVES 4

2 trimmed racks of lamb (about 2 pounds each)

5 tablespoons extra virgin olive oil

3 tablespoons chopped mixed fresh herbs (rosemary, thyme, and/or marjoram, in any combination)

Salt and freshly ground black pepper

POLENTA

1^1/$_2$ cups water

^{1}/$_2$ cup polenta

^{1}/$_4$ cup cloves roasted garlic (see page 5), with the cooking oil

3 tablespoons unsalted butter

Salt and freshly ground black pepper

MUSTARD SAUCE

^{1}/$_4$ cup Dijon mustard

2 tablespoons white wine

^{1}/$_3$ cup lamb cooking juices

1 tablespoon fresh baby soft thyme

TO MARINATE THE LAMB: Rub the lamb with 3 tablespoons of the olive oil, sprinkle with 2 tablespoons of the herbs, and marinate overnight.

TO PREPARE THE POLENTA: Bring the water to a boil in a medium saucepan and slowly add the polenta. Simmer over low heat, stirring occasionally, for 30 minutes, or until done. Purée the roasted garlic with the cooking oil until smooth. Mix 2 tablespoons of the butter and all of the garlic into the polenta and season to taste with salt and pepper. Spread the mixture into a plastic wrap–lined 8-inch square pan and refrigerate for 2 hours.

TO COOK THE LAMB: Preheat the oven to 450°. Heat a large ovenproof pan over medium-high heat, add the remaining 2 tablespoons olive oil, and sear the lamb on all sides. Roast in the oven for 8 to 12 minutes, or until slightly less than the desired degree of doneness. Remove the pan from the oven and allow the lamb to rest for 5 minutes. Slice each rack between the bones just prior to serving, and season to taste with salt and pepper. Reserve the lamb juices.

TO COOK THE POLENTA: Cut the polenta into four 3-inch circles. Cook the polenta in the remaining 1 tablespoon butter in a medium sauté pan over medium-high heat for 3 minutes on each side, or until golden brown and crispy.

continued

TO PREPARE THE MUSTARD SAUCE: Combine the mustard, white wine, and lamb juices in a bowl. Whisk until well blended.

Place a crispy polenta circle in the center of each plate. Fan the sliced lamb on one edge of the polenta, and spoon the sauce around the plates. Garnish with baby thyme.

Polenta is the Italian word for cornmeal. It is more finely ground than regular cornmeal, but if you can't find polenta, cornmeal or grits will work just as well.

Peppered Lamb Loin with
Mustard Spaetzle and Thyme Reduction

6 tablespoons extra virgin olive oil

4 tablespoons cracked
black pepper

4 cloves garlic, sliced

$1/2$ teaspoon cumin seeds,
coarsely ground

$1/2$ cup thyme sprigs

1 pound trimmed lamb loin

SPAETZLE

1 cup flour

$1/2$ teaspoon salt

$1/4$ teaspoon freshly
ground black pepper

$1^{1}/_{2}$ teaspoons whole-grain mustard

$1^{1}/_{2}$ teaspoons Dijon mustard

1 egg, beaten

$1/4$ to $1/2$ cup milk

2 tablespoons unsalted butter

$1^{1}/_{2}$ tablespoons chopped
fresh parsley

$3/4$ cup meat stock reduction
(see page 4)

Salt and freshly ground
black pepper

TO MARINATE THE LAMB: Combine 4 tablespoons of the olive oil, the cracked pepper, garlic, cumin, and thyme sprigs, reserving 1 thyme sprig for the sauces, in a large, resealable plastic bag. Add the lamb loin, seal closed, and marinate overnight in the refrigerator.

TO PREPARE THE SPAETZLE: Combine the flour, salt, pepper, whole-grain and Dijon mustards, and egg in a medium bowl. Add enough of the milk to form a somewhat stiff batter. Cover and refrigerate the batter for at least 1 hour.

Bring a large pot of salted water to a boil. Use the back of a spoon to press the dough through a spaetzle maker or funnel into the boiling water. Cook for 1 minute, or until the spaetzle begin to float. Drain, place in a small bowl, and toss with the butter and parsley. Keep warm.

TO PREPARE THE LAMB: Preheat the oven to 450°. Heat the remaining 2 tablespoons olive oil in a roasting pan on the stove top over medium-high heat. Sear the lamb for 2 to 3 minutes on each side, or until browned. Roast in the oven for 8 to 10 minutes, or until cooked to the desired degree of doneness. Remove from the oven and let rest for 5 minutes. Cut into 16 slices just prior to serving.

continued

TO PREPARE THE SAUCE: Bring the meat stock reduction to a simmer in a small saucepan and add the reserved thyme sprig. Simmer for 1 minute, remove the thyme, and season to taste with salt and pepper.

Spoon some of the spaetzle onto the center of each plate. Fan 4 lamb slices slightly overlapping one side of the spaetzle, and spoon the sauce around the plates.

Spaetzle—irregular-shaped noodles—has its origin in Germany and Austria. It is the simplest type of pasta to make at home because it doesn't involve any rolling. For this recipe I have flavored the spaetzle with mustard, but it can be left plain or flavored with any type of herb or spice. Spaetzle is also wonderful sautéed in a little butter, after it is boiled, to crisp it up.

Yukon Gold Potato and
Braised Oxtail Tarts

SERVES 4

OXTAILS

2 tablespoons canola oil

8 oxtails

1 large yellow onion, chopped

1 carrot, peeled and chopped

1 stalk celery, chopped

4 cloves garlic, chopped

1 tomato, seeded and coarsely chopped

1 cup red wine

3 cups chicken stock (see page 4)

1 bay leaf

2 sprigs thyme

Salt and freshly ground black pepper

DOUGH

1¹/₂ cups flour

1 teaspoon salt

1 cup cold unsalted butter, chopped

¹/₃ cup ice water

1 Yukon Gold potato, peeled

Salt and freshly ground black pepper

¹/₄ cup heavy cream

1 egg yolk, whisked with 1 tablespoon water

TO BRAISE THE OXTAILS: Preheat the oven to 325°. Heat the canola oil in a small roasting pan on the stove top over medium-high heat, add the oxtails, and sear for 3 minutes on each side, or until golden brown. Remove the oxtails and set aside. Add the onion, carrot, celery, garlic, and tomato and cook for 7 to 10 minutes, or until golden brown and caramelized. Add the oxtails, red wine, stock, bay leaf, and thyme to the pan. Season with salt and pepper, cover tightly, and braise in the oven for 3 hours.

TO PREPARE THE DOUGH: Place the flour, salt, and butter in a medium bowl. Using a pastry cutter or fork, cut the butter into the flour until it forms pea-sized pieces. Add the water and mix with a fork until the dough just comes together (it should have visible streaks of butter). Form the dough into a disk, wrap in plastic wrap, and refrigerate for at least 1 hour.

TO PREPARE THE TART: Bring a large pot of salted water to a boil. Slice the potato into ¹/₈-inch-thick disks and cook in the boiling water for 5 minutes. Remove the potato slices from the water, being careful not to break them, and set aside.

Strain the braising liquid from the oxtails through a fine-mesh sieve and set aside. Remove the meat from the bones, shred, and place the meat in a medium bowl. Season to taste with salt and pepper.

On a floured surface, roll out the dough ¹/₈ inch thick and cut out 8 circles large enough to line and cover a 3-inch-diameter by ¹/₂-inch-high tartlet ring. Place 4 tartlet rings on a parchment-lined baking sheet, and press a dough circle into each one.

continued

Place the cream in a small bowl and add the potato slices. Remove some of the potatoes from the cream and form a layer of potato in the bottom of each tart. Season with salt and pepper. Spoon some of the shredded oxtail into each tart, cover with 2 layers of potatoes, and press down firmly. Mound the remaining oxtail onto the tarts, cover with the remaining dough, and seal the edges, trimming any excess. Refrigerate for at least 30 minutes.

Preheat the oven to 375°. Brush the tops of the tarts with the egg, sprinkle with salt and pepper, and bake for 35 to 40 minutes, or until golden brown.

Meanwhile, cook the reserved braising liquid in a small saucepan over medium heat for 20 to 30 minutes, or until reduced to about $1\frac{1}{2}$ cups. Season to taste with salt and pepper.

Remove the tarts from the oven, let stand for 5 minutes, and cut in half. Spoon some of the sauce in the center of each plate and place 2 tart halves on the sauce to form a **V**.

At one time, oxtail was meat from an ox, hence the name. Although it is still called oxtail, what you are buying now is actually beef. Oxtail can be extremely tough and requires long, slow braising, but the result is rich, incredibly succulent meat. If you have the time, decrease the temperature to 225° and let it cook all day, or up to 12 hours. The meat will be even more tender and luscious. The oxtails can be braised a day or two ahead.

This dish can also be prepared in a 9-inch tart pan by cutting out 2 dough circles each 12 inches in diameter. Layer the ingredients as directed. The cooking time may be a little longer.

vegetables

151 | Open-Faced Wild Mushroom Tarts with Braised Leeks and Red Wine Emulsion

153 | Tomato Risotto with Caramelized Onion Purée

154 | Goat Cheese and Basil Ravioli with Tomato Water

156 | Butternut Squash Ravioli with Brown Butter–Citrus Vinaigrette

158 | Vegetable "Lasagna" with Roasted Garlic Broth

160 | Whole Roasted Tomatoes with Wild Mushroom–Strewn Quinoa

162 | Potato Gnocchi with Oven-Roasted Tomatoes, Pearl Onions, and Goat Cheese

164 | Spring Pea Risotto with Spicy Herb Sauce

Open-Faced Wild Mushroom Tarts with Braised Leeks and Red Wine Emulsion

SERVES 6

TART SHELLS

3/4 cup all-purpose flour

1/2 teaspoon salt

1/2 cup cold unsalted butter, chopped

3 tablespoons ice water

EMULSION

1 shallot, chopped

1 tablespoon plus 1/4 cup unsalted butter

1/2 small tomato, seeded and diced

2 tablespoons balsamic vinegar (see note, page 130)

1 1/2 cups red wine

Salt and freshly ground black pepper

LEEKS

1 leek (white part only), cut into 1/4-inch-thick disks

2 tablespoons unsalted butter

1 cup chicken stock (see page 4)

Salt and freshly ground black pepper

2 cups mixed roasted mushrooms (see page 5), with the cooking liquid

1 tablespoon tiny sage leaves

TO PREPARE THE TART SHELLS: Place the flour, salt, and butter in a medium bowl. Using a pastry cutter or fork, cut the butter into the flour until it forms pea-size pieces. Add the water and mix with a fork until the dough just comes together (it should have visible streaks of butter). Form into a disk, wrap in plastic wrap, and refrigerate for at least 1 hour.

Preheat the oven to 350°. On a floured surface, roll out the dough 1/8 inch thick and cut out 6 circles large enough to line a 3-inch-diameter by 1/2-inch-high tartlet ring. Place 6 tartlet rings on a parchment-lined baking sheet, and press a dough circle into each one, trimming any excess. (Alternatively, use an 8- or 9-inch tart pan.) Line the tarts with parchment paper and fill with pastry weights or dried beans to prevent the dough from bubbling or shrinking. Bake for 15 minutes, or until golden brown. Cool the tart shells on the pan, and then carefully remove the tartlet rings, weights, and parchment.

TO PREPARE THE EMULSION: Cook the shallot with the 1 tablespoon butter in a small saucepan over medium heat for 3 to 4 minutes, or until translucent. Add the tomato and balsamic vinegar and cook for 2 minutes, or until reduced to a glaze. Add the red wine and cook for 20 minutes, or until reduced to 1/2 cup. Stir in the 1/4 cup butter and season to taste with salt and pepper. Froth with a handheld blender or mixer set at high speed just prior to serving.

TO PREPARE THE LEEKS: Cook the leek and the butter in a medium saucepan over medium-low heat for 10 minutes, or until translucent. Add the stock and cook over medium-low heat for 30 minutes, or until the leek is very soft and most of the liquid is absorbed. Season with salt and pepper.

continued

TO PREPARE THE MUSHROOMS: Cut the mushrooms into bite-sized pieces and place in a small saucepan with their cooking liquid. Cook over medium heat for 5 minutes, or until warm. Season to taste with salt and pepper.

Place a tart shell in the center of each plate and spoon in some of the leeks. Mound the mushrooms over the leeks and spoon the emulsion over the mushrooms and around the plate. Garnish with tiny sage leaves.

Handheld blenders are great little tools to have around. They are inexpensive and are ideal for emulsifying or frothing sauces, puréeing soups or sauces right in the pot, and even work well as a bar blender. If you don't have a handheld blender, an electric mixer set at the highest speed will give you similar results.

Tomato Risotto with Caramelized Onion Purée

TOMATO WATER

12 large beefsteak tomatoes

1 tablespoon salt

ONION PURÉE

1 large yellow onion, chopped

2 tablespoons unsalted butter

1/2 cup chicken stock (see page 4)

Salt and freshly ground
black pepper

2 shallots, minced

2 tablespoons unsalted butter

1 cup arborio rice

2 tablespoons tomato paste

3 tablespoons chopped
oil-packed sun-dried tomato

1/4 cup peeled, seeded, and
chopped fresh tomato

Salt and freshly ground
black pepper

1 tablespoon finely chopped
fresh basil

TO PREPARE THE TOMATO WATER: Purée the beefsteak tomatoes and add the salt. Pour the purée into a cheesecloth-lined sieve set in a large bowl and refrigerate for 8 hours, or until all of the juices have dripped from the purée. Discard the solids.

TO PREPARE THE ONION PURÉE: Cook the onion with the butter in a small sauté pan over medium heat for 10 to 12 minutes, or until the onion is caramelized. Purée the onion and stock until smooth, season to taste with salt and pepper, and keep warm.

TO PREPARE THE RISOTTO: Cook the shallots and the butter in a large sauté pan over medium heat for 8 to 10 minutes, or until golden brown and caramelized. Add the rice and cook for 2 minutes, stirring frequently. Slowly add 1/4 cup of the tomato water and stir until completely absorbed. Add the remaining tomato water 1/4 cup at a time, stirring continuously with a smooth, gentle motion until the liquid is completely absorbed. (The risotto will take 40 to 50 minutes to cook completely.) Add the tomato paste to the rice about halfway through cooking. Stir in the sun-dried and fresh tomato at the end of cooking, and season to taste with salt and pepper.

Spoon some of the risotto in the center of each plate and drizzle the onion purée over the risotto and around the plate. Sprinkle the basil over the risotto.

> The tomato water adds a fresh tomato flavor to this risotto,
> but if you are short on time, chicken stock can be substituted.

Goat Cheese and Basil Ravioli with Tomato Water

SERVES 4

TOMATO WATER

10 beefsteak tomatoes, chopped

Salt and freshly ground
black pepper

RAVIOLI

4 ounces soft goat cheese
(see note, page 35)

2 tablespoons chopped fresh basil

2 tablespoons minced shallots

2 tablespoons chopped
fresh chives

Salt and freshly ground
black pepper

32 3-inch square wonton
skins (see note, page 157)

1 egg, lightly beaten

12 red teardrop tomatoes,
peeled and blanched

4 yellow teardrop tomatoes,
peeled and blanched

1 tablespoon tiny red basil shoots

1 tablespoon tiny green basil shoots

TO PREPARE THE TOMATO WATER: Purée the tomatoes and season with salt. Pour the purée into a cheesecloth-lined sieve set in a large bowl and refrigerate for 8 hours, or until all of the juices have dripped from the purée.

Discard the solids from the tomato purée and place the tomato water in a small saucepan. Cook over medium heat for 5 to 7 minutes, or until warm. Season to taste with salt and pepper.

TO PREPARE THE RAVIOLI FILLING: Place the goat cheese, chopped basil, shallots, and chives in a medium bowl and mix until combined. Season to taste with salt and pepper.

TO PREPARE THE RAVIOLI: Bring a pot of salted water to a boil. Place a wonton skin on a flat work surface and spoon 1 tablespoon of the filling in the center. Lightly brush the edges with the egg and top with another wonton skin. Firmly press the edges of the wontons to seal. Repeat the process with the remaining ingredients. (The ravioli can be prepared to this point several hours in advance and refrigerated on a floured sheet pan.) Cook the ravioli in the boiling water for 3 minutes, or until al dente, then drain.

Place 4 ravioli in each shallow bowl and ladle 3 red tomatoes, 1 yellow tomato, and tomato water over each bowl. Sprinkle red and green basil shoots over the ravioli and top with freshly ground black pepper.

> If you want to make authentic ravioli, you can make your own pasta. Combine 2 cups semolina flour with 3 lightly beaten eggs until the dough comes together. Refrigerate the dough for 1 hour, roll out the dough $1/16$ inch thick, and cut into squares.

Butternut Squash Ravioli with Brown Butter–Citrus Vinaigrette

SERVES 4

RAVIOLI

1 small butternut squash

1 tablespoon canola oil

$1/2$ teaspoon ground cinnamon

$1/4$ teaspoon ground nutmeg

2 teaspoons sugar

Salt and freshly ground
black pepper

40 small wonton skins,
trimmed to 2-inch squares

1 egg, lightly beaten

VINAIGRETTE

$1/2$ cup unsalted butter

2 tablespoons sliced almonds

2 tablespoons freshly
squeezed orange juice

1 tablespoon freshly
squeezed lemon juice

1 teaspoon minced orange zest

Salt and freshly ground
black pepper

3 cups fresh spinach leaves,
cleaned and stemmed

Freshly ground black pepper

TO PREPARE THE RAVIOLI FILLING: Preheat the oven to 350°. Cut the squash in half and scoop out the seeds. Rub the flesh with the oil and season with the cinnamon and nutmeg. Place the squash halves, cut side down, on a rimmed baking sheet and add $1/4$ inch of water to the pan. Roast for 45 minutes, or until tender.

Remove the squash from the oven, cool, and scrape out the flesh. Purée the flesh and sugar until smooth, and season to taste with salt and pepper.

TO PREPARE THE RAVIOLI: Place a wonton skin on a flat work surface and spoon 1 tablespoon of the squash filling in the center. Brush the edges with the egg and top with another wonton skin. Firmly press the edges of the wontons to seal. Repeat the process with the remaining ingredients. (The ravioli can be prepared to this point several hours in advance and refrigerated on a floured sheet pan.)

TO PREPARE THE VINAIGRETTE: Cook the butter in a small saucepan over medium heat for 5 minutes, or until dark brown with a nutty aroma. Remove from the heat, add the almonds, orange juice, lemon juice, and orange zest and season to taste with salt and pepper.

TO COOK THE RAVIOLI: Bring a large pot of salted water to a boil. Cook the ravioli in the boiling water for 3 to 4 minutes, or until al dente, then drain.

Meanwhile, prepare the spinach by placing it in a hot sauté pan over medium-high heat with one-third of the vinaigrette. Quickly wilt, and season to taste with salt and pepper.

Place some of the spinach in the center of each plate and top with 5 ravioli. Spoon some of the remaining vinaigrette over the ravioli and top with freshly ground black pepper.

Wonton skins can be found in the produce section of most grocery stores. They usually can be found in 3- and 6-inch squares, and occasionally in 3-inch circles. They can be cut to any size you desire and are a great substitute for fresh pasta in ravioli and tortellini.

Vegetable "Lasagna"
with Roasted Garlic Broth

SERVES 4

LASAGNA

2 large potatoes, peeled and
thinly sliced lengthwise

Salt and freshly ground
black pepper

1/2 cup freshly grated
Parmesan cheese

4 roasted red bell peppers
(see page 5), cut into wide strips

2 yellow squashes, cut lengthwise
into 1/4-inch-thick slices

4 roasted yellow bell peppers
(see page 5), cut into wide strips

2 zucchini, cut lengthwise into
1/4-inch-thick slices

4 ounces mozzarella cheese,
thinly sliced

BROTH

1 bulb roasted garlic (see page 5),
with the cooking oil

3 cups chicken stock (see page 4)

Salt and freshly ground
black pepper

1 tablespoon extra virgin olive oil

1 tablespoon finely minced chives

TO PREPARE THE LASAGNA: Preheat the oven to 350°. Generously butter an 8-inch square baking pan. Using one-third of the potatoes, form a layer in the pan. Season lightly with salt and pepper and sprinkle with some of the Parmesan cheese. Using half of the red bell peppers, form a layer on the potatoes, followed by layers of half the yellow squash, yellow bell pepper, and zucchini, in that order. Top with one-third of the potatoes and layer all of the remaining vegetables in the same order as before. Top with a final layer of potatoes and the mozzarella cheese. Bake uncovered for 1 hour, or until the cheese is golden brown. Remove from the oven and let stand for 15 minutes. Cut 4 3-inch squares from the center of the pan; reserve the edges for another use.

TO PREPARE THE BROTH: Squeeze the garlic from the garlic bulb and purée with the reserved garlic oil until smooth. Slowly add the stock and purée until smooth. Pour the broth into a medium saucepan and cook over medium heat for 5 minutes, or until warm. Season to taste with salt and pepper.

Place a piece of the lasagna in the center of each bowl and ladle in the broth. Top with freshly ground black pepper and drizzle extra virgin olive oil around the dish. Finish with a spray of minced chives.

> I use potatoes instead of pasta to help keep the lasagna a little lighter. This dish can be prepared a day ahead, which makes it a perfect dish to serve to guests. It also makes a wonderful side dish when served in smaller portions. If serving as a side dish, use 3/4 cup reduced chicken stock and 5 cloves roasted garlic to make a thicker sauce and spoon it over the lasagna.

Whole Roasted Tomatoes with Wild Mushroom–Strewn Quinoa

SERVES 4

TOMATOES

8 tomatoes

3 tablespoons extra virgin olive oil

8 cloves garlic

8 sprigs thyme

8 sprigs tarragon

8 bay leaves

8 large fresh basil leaves

QUINOA

2 cups water

1 teaspoon canola oil

$^1/_2$ cup quinoa (see note, page 60)

1 shallot, finely diced

2 tablespoons unsalted butter

$^3/_4$ cup mixed wild mushrooms (such as shiitake, oyster, or portobello), cleaned and cut into bite-sized pieces

Salt and freshly ground black pepper

1 tablespoon plus $^1/_4$ cup extra virgin olive oil

2 tablespoons balsamic vinegar (see note, page 130)

Salt and freshly ground black pepper

TO PREPARE THE TOMATOES: Preheat the oven to 325°. Bring a large pot of salted water to a boil. Cut a small **X** in the bottom of each tomato, blanch in the boiling water, and peel. Cut a $^3/_4$-inch slice off the bottom of each tomato, reserving the pieces for lids. Scoop out the seeds and the center flesh of the tomatoes and discard. Rub the insides with the olive oil and place a clove of garlic, a sprig of thyme, a sprig of tarragon, a bay leaf, and a basil leaf in each tomato. Place the tomatoes in a roasting pan and place the lids on top to cover. Roast for 10 to 12 minutes, or until the tomatoes just begin to soften. Remove the garlic and herbs and discard, reserving the tomato lids. Keep the tomatoes in the pan.

TO PREPARE THE QUINOA: Bring the water to a boil in a medium saucepan. Meanwhile, heat the canola oil in a medium sauté pan over medium heat. Add the quinoa and cook, stirring frequently, for 5 minutes, or until it has a nutty aroma. Stir the quinoa into the boiling water and bring to a simmer. Cover and cook over medium-low heat for 15 minutes, or until most of the liquid is absorbed. Remove from the heat, cover tightly, and let stand for 15 minutes.

Cook the shallot with the butter in a small sauté pan over medium heat for 2 to 3 minutes, or until translucent. Add the mushrooms and cook for 5 to 7 minutes, or until tender. Stir in the quinoa, season to taste with salt and pepper, and remove from the heat.

TO PREPARE THE STUFFED TOMATOES: Spoon the warm quinoa mixture into the hot tomatoes and top with the lids. Rub the outside of the tomatoes with the 1 tablespoon olive oil, and return them to the oven for 5 minutes.

TO PREPARE THE SAUCE: Purée the tomato tops with the balsamic vinegar and the $1/4$ cup olive oil, and season to taste with salt and pepper.

Place 2 tomatoes in the center of each plate, and spoon the sauce over the tomatoes and around the plate.

Extra virgin olive oil comes from the first pressing of the olives. It has perfect color, flavor, and aroma. Virgin or pure olive oil comes from the second pressing and is not as intensely flavored as the first pressing.

This is a light entrée. If it's too light for you, add any type of steamed fish; it would be great drizzled with this sauce.

Potato Gnocchi with Oven-Roasted Tomatoes, Pearl Onions, and Goat Cheese

SERVES 4

TOMATOES

3 large ripe tomatoes

2 tablespoons extra virgin olive oil

Salt and freshly ground black pepper

4 sprigs thyme

2 sprigs rosemary

VINAIGRETTE

1 tablespoon balsamic vinegar (see note, page 130)

1½ teaspoons fresh thyme leaves

3 tablespoons extra virgin olive oil

Salt and freshly ground black pepper

TO PREPARE THE TOMATOES: Preheat the oven to 225°. Slice the tomatoes ½ inch thick and lay on a wire rack set in a baking pan. Drizzle the tomatoes with the olive oil and season lightly with salt and pepper. Arrange the thyme and rosemary sprigs over the tomatoes and bake for 3 hours.

TO PREPARE THE VINAIGRETTE: Place the balsamic vinegar and thyme leaves in a small bowl and whisk in the olive oil. Season to taste with salt and pepper.

TO PREPARE THE GNOCCHI: In a large bowl, rice the potatoes or finely mash with a fork. Work the yolks into the potato and knead in 1 cup of flour, adding additional flour as needed to form a dough that is not too sticky. Season with salt and pepper.

Divide the mixture into 4 portions and roll each portion into a long cigar shape about ½ inch in diameter. Cut each roll into ½-inch pieces and delicately pinch the pieces in the middle. Place on a lightly floured pan and refrigerate until ready to cook.

TO PREPARE THE ONIONS: Cook the onions and butter in a medium sauté pan over medium heat for 15 minutes, or until the onions are golden brown and tender. Add the roasted tomatoes and cook for 2 to 3 minutes, or until the tomatoes are warm. Season to taste with salt and pepper.

GNOCCHI

2 large Idaho potatoes, baked and peeled

2 egg yolks

1 to 1¹/₂ cups flour

Salt and freshly ground black pepper

ONIONS

24 pearl onions, peeled

2 tablespoons unsalted butter

Salt and freshly ground black pepper

1 tablespoon fresh thyme leaves

5 ounces soft goat cheese (see note, page 35)

MEANWHILE, COOK THE GNOCCHI: Bring a large pot of salted water to a boil. Add the gnocchi and cook for 2 to 3 minutes, or until they float. Remove them from the pan with a slotted spoon and place in a large bowl. Add the onion mixture and toss until combined.

Spoon some of the gnocchi mixture in the center of each plate and sprinkle with the thyme and goat cheese. Drizzle the vinaigrette over the gnocchi and around the plates.

> This dish may seem complicated, but it actually requires very little last-minute preparation, making it a perfect dish to serve to guests. The tomatoes can be prepared up to a day ahead and refrigerated in an airtight container. The gnocchi can be prepared several hours ahead and cooked just prior to serving.

Spring Pea Risotto
with Spicy Herb Sauce

SERVES 4

SAUCE

1 bunch fresh flat-leaf parsley

4 tablespoons canola oil

2 tablespoons ice water

2 teaspoons togarashi

1 tablespoon minced jalapeño chile

Salt and freshly ground
black pepper

2 shallots, minced

2 tablespoons unsalted butter

1 cup arborio rice

4 cups chicken stock
(see page 4)

1 cup shelled fresh spring
peas, blanched

TO PREPARE THE SAUCE: Sauté the parsley in 1 tablespoon of the canola oil in a hot sauté pan for 10 seconds. Remove immediately, transfer to a small bowl, and refrigerate until cooled. Coarsely chop the parsley and purée with the ice water and the remaining 3 tablespoons of the canola oil until smooth. Strain through a fine-mesh sieve. Whisk in the togarashi and jalapeño and season to taste with salt and pepper.

TO PREPARE THE RISOTTO: Cook the shallots and butter in a large sauté pan over medium heat for 2 to 3 minutes, or until translucent. Add the rice and cook for 2 minutes, stirring frequently. Slowly add $1/4$ cup of the stock and stir until completely absorbed. Add the remaining stock $1/4$ cup at a time, stirring continuously with a smooth, gentle motion until the liquid is completely absorbed. (The risotto will take 40 to 50 minutes to cook completely.) Add the peas with the final addition of stock. Fold in half of the sauce and season to taste with salt and pepper.

Spoon some of the risotto in the center of each plate and drizzle the remaining sauce over the risotto and around the plate.

Togarashi is a combination of spices used in Japanese cooking. It is available in Asian markets, but if you can't find it, you can make your own. Grind 1 teaspoon black sesame seeds, 1 teaspoon paprika, $1/2$ teaspoon dried basil, $1/2$ teaspoon ground bay leaves, $1/2$ teaspoon Szechuan pepper, $1/2$ teaspoon cayenne pepper, 1 teaspoon dried red chiles, $1/2$ teaspoon sea salt, and $1/2$ teaspoon orange zest in a blender for 2 minutes, or until finely ground. This can be kept in an airtight container for up to 6 months.

DESSERTS
sorbets | pastries | cakes

soups, sorbets, and granités

167 | Chilled Ginger-Melon Soup with Citrus Granité

168 | Warm Apple Cider Soup with Crispy Apple Turnovers

169 | Chilled Apricot Soup with Vanilla Bean Ice Cream
and Almond Shortbread

171 | Poached Peaches with Champagne Granité

172 | Chilled Peach Soup with Lemongrass Sorbet

174 | Warm Bing Cherries with White Chocolate–
Bing Cherry Sorbet

175 | Warm Berry Compote with Vanilla Frozen Yogurt

Chilled Ginger-Melon Soup
with Citrus Granité

SERVES 4

SOUP

2 small, very ripe honeydew
melons, peeled, halved, seeded,
and chopped

2 tablespoons preserved ginger
(see page 6)

GRANITÉ

1 grapefruit

2 lemons

2 oranges

¼ cup simple syrup (see page 6)

TO PREPARE THE SOUP: Purée the melon and preserved ginger until smooth. Pour the mixture into a cheesecloth-lined sieve set into a large bowl and let drain overnight in the refrigerator. Discard the pulp and keep the soup refrigerated until ready to serve.

TO PREPARE THE GRANITÉ: Juice the grapefruit, lemons, and oranges and strain through a fine-mesh sieve. Pour the juice into a shallow pan, stir in the simple syrup, and freeze. To form the granité, scrape the mixture with a spoon every 15 to 20 minutes for 2 hours, or until frozen.

Spoon some of the granité in the center of each bowl and gently spoon in the soup.

> *Granité* is the French word for what Americans would call an "ice." It is a combination of juice, sugar, and water that is stirred during the freezing process to form the finely granulated ice. I prefer to scrape the liquid with a spoon, as it freezes to form a flakier granité. If time gets away from you and the granité freezes too hard to scrape, you can let it melt and start over with no adverse effects.

Warm Apple Cider Soup
with Crispy Apple Turnovers

SERVES 6

SOUP

6 cups apple cider

1 cinnamon stick

½ cup granulated sugar

3 tablespoons freshly squeezed lemon juice

1 tablespoon orange zest

2 whole allspice berries

FILLING

1 cup peeled, cored, and diced Granny Smith apple

2 tablespoons freshly squeezed lemon juice

¼ cup flour

¼ teaspoon ground cinnamon

3 sheets filo dough

6 tablespoons unsalted butter, melted

4 tablespoons confectioners' sugar

TO MAKE THE SOUP: Cook all of the ingredients in a large saucepan over medium heat for 30 minutes, or until reduced by half. Strain through a fine-mesh sieve and set aside. Warm before serving.

TO PREPARE THE FILLING: Place the apples in a small bowl and toss with the lemon juice until well coated. Drain the excess lemon juice, add the flour and cinnamon, and toss.

TO MAKE THE TURNOVERS: Preheat the oven to 350°. Lay a sheet of filo out, brush with 2 tablespoons of the melted butter, and sprinkle with 2 tablespoons of the confectioners' sugar. Top with a sheet of filo and repeat the process. Place the last sheet of filo on the stack and brush with the remaining butter. Cut the filo lengthwise into 6 3-inch-wide strips. Turn the strips over so the buttered side is facing down, and place a spoonful of the filling mixture at the end of 1 strip. Fold over a bottom corner diagonally to form a triangle. (The bottom edge should align with the side edge.) Continue folding the triangle in alternating directions to the end of the strip. Repaet the process with the remaining strips. Place on a baking sheet and bake for 15 to 20 minutes, or until golden brown.

Place a warm apple turnover in the center of each bowl and pour the warm soup around the turnover.

Filo is a dough rolled paper thin. When you open a package of filo sheets, unroll them and immediately cover with a damp paper towel to prevent them from drying out. Each time you take a sheet, cover the remainder promptly. Filo dough is available in the freezer section of most grocery stores. It is also spelled "fillo" or "phyllo," so don't be confused, they are all the same.

Chilled Apricot Soup
with Vanilla Bean Ice Cream
and Almond Shortbread

SERVES 8

ICE CREAM

2 cups heavy cream

1 vanilla bean

4 egg yolks

6 tablespoons sugar

SHORTBREAD

1 cup unsalted butter, at
room temperature

$^1/_2$ cup confectioners' sugar

2 teaspoons pure vanilla extract

Pinch of salt

2 cups cake flour

$^1/_2$ cup finely ground almonds

$^1/_4$ cup slivered almonds

SOUP

$^3/_4$ cup sugar

$^1/_4$ cup water

6 apricots, pitted and coarsely
chopped

$^1/_2$ cup freshly squeezed
orange juice, warmed

TO PREPARE THE ICE CREAM: Fill a large bowl halfway with ice and cold water. Place the cream in a medium saucepan. Split the vanilla bean lengthwise and, using the back of a knife, scrape the seeds into the cream. Add the pod to the pan and bring the cream to a boil. Whisk together the egg yolks and sugar in a small bowl and slowly whisk in some of the hot cream mixture to temper the eggs. Pour the egg mixture into the cream and cook over medium heat for 2 to 3 minutes, or until the mixture coats the back of a spoon and steam rises from the surface. Strain into a medium bowl through a fine-mesh sieve and cool in the ice-water bath, stirring occasionally, until chilled. Freeze in an ice cream machine and keep frozen until ready to use.

TO PREPARE THE SHORTBREAD: Line a baking sheet with parchment paper. Using an electric mixer or by hand, cream the butter and confectioner's sugar in a large bowl. Add the vanilla and salt and mix well. Add the flour and ground almonds and mix until fully incorporated. Spread the dough into a $^1/_2$-inch-thick layer on the baking sheet, sprinkle with the slivered almonds, and gently press them into the dough. Refrigerate for 30 minutes.

Preheat the oven to 350°. Remove the parchment and dough from the pan and place on a flat surface. Cut the dough into 2-inch circles and place them on the baking sheet. Bake for 12 to 15 minutes, or until the bottom edges just start to brown. Remove from the oven and cool on the pan.

continued

TO PREPARE THE SOUP: Cook the sugar and water in a small, heavy-bottomed sauté pan over medium heat for 5 minutes, or until lightly golden. Do not stir the sugar, or it may crystallize (see note, page 183).

Add the apricots and stir until coated. Add the orange juice and simmer, stirring frequently, for 2 to 3 minutes to dissolve any hardened sugar. Remove from the heat, let the mixture cool slightly, and then purée until smooth. Strain into a bowl through a fine-mesh sieve and refrigerate until ready to use. Thin with a little water if necessary.

Place a cookie in the center of each bowl, top with a small scoop of ice cream, and spoon in some of the soup.

This is a wonderful dish for summer, when apricots are at the height of their season. If apricots aren't available, plums would also work well, but peel them before adding them to the sugar.

Poached Peaches with Champagne Granité

SERVES 6

PEACHES

8 ripe peaches, peeled and pitted

2 cups water

½ cup freshly squeezed lemon juice

1 cup sugar

1 cup champagne

TO PREPARE THE PEACHES: Chop 4 of the peaches and purée with the water and lemon juice for 2 minutes, or until smooth. Add the sugar and pour the mixture into a saucepan. Cut each of the remaining 4 peaches into 12 slices. Place the peach slices in the saucepan and simmer for 10 minutes, or until tender. Using a slotted spoon, remove the peach slices from the pan and set aside. Reserve the cooking liquid.

TO PREPARE THE GRANITÉ: Combine the champagne and 1 cup of the reserved cooking liquid in a shallow pan and place in the freezer. To form the granité, scrape the mixture with a spoon every 15 to 20 minutes for 2 hours, or until frozen.

Fan the peach slices in the center of each plate. Spoon the granité on the bottom edge of the fan and drizzle some of the reserved liquid onto the plate.

> When purchasing the champagne for the granité, don't skimp. You don't need to break the bank, but the quality of the champagne will definitely affect the final product. Use a moderately priced, good-quality champagne or sparkling wine, and save the remainder to enjoy with your guests.

Chilled Peach Soup
with Lemongrass Sorbet

SERVES 4

SOUP

6 peaches, peeled, pitted, and chopped

$^2/_3$ cup freshly squeezed orange juice

$^2/_3$ cup simple syrup (see page 6)

SORBET

$1^1/_2$ cups apple juice

$^1/_4$ cup freshly squeezed lemon juice

$^1/_2$ cup chopped lemongrass

1 tablespoon corn syrup

$^1/_4$ cup simple syrup (see page 6)

$^1/_2$ cup peeled and finely diced peaches

TO PREPARE THE SOUP: Purée the peaches, orange juice, and simple syrup until smooth. Pour into a cheesecloth-lined sieve set into a large bowl and drain overnight in the refrigerator. Discard the pulp and keep the soup refrigerated until ready to serve.

TO PREPARE THE SORBET: Bring the apple and lemon juices to a boil in a medium saucepan and remove from the heat. Add the lemongrass, cover, and steep, off the heat, for 30 minutes. Strain into a medium bowl through a fine-mesh sieve and stir in the corn syrup and simple syrup. Refrigerate until thoroughly chilled and then freeze in an ice cream machine. Keep frozen until ready to use.

Place a scoop of sorbet in the center of each bowl. Sprinkle the diced peaches around the sorbet and spoon the soup into the bowls.

> Lemongrass, a popular ingredient in Thai cooking, is a tall, stalky herb with a strong lemon flavor and fragrance. If you can't find lemongrass, lemon balm will work as well. Otherwise, make lemon sorbet by combining $1^1/_2$ cups simple syrup, $^3/_4$ cup freshly squeezed lemon juice, and 1 tablespoon corn syrup and freezing it in an ice cream machine.

Warm Bing Cherries with White Chocolate–Bing Cherry Sorbet

SERVES 4

SORBET

7 ounces white chocolate, coarsely chopped

1/3 cup corn syrup

1 cup warm water

1/2 cup pitted, quartered Bing cherries

SAUCE

2 tablespoons sugar

1 tablespoon freshly squeezed lemon juice

1 cup water

2 cups pitted, quartered Bing cherries

TO PREPARE THE SORBET: Prepare a double boiler with barely simmering water. Melt the white chocolate and corn syrup in the top of the double boiler. Whisk in the water, remove from the heat, and cool. Freeze in an ice cream machine, and then fold in the cherries. Keep frozen until ready to use.

TO PREPARE THE SAUCE: Bring the sugar, lemon juice, and water to a boil in a small saucepan over medium heat. Add the cherries and simmer over medium heat for 5 minutes, or until warm.

Spoon some of the sauce into the center of each plate and top with a scoop of sorbet.

> This recipe is a wonderful way to showcase seasonal fruits. The smooth sweetness of the white chocolate sorbet is the perfect backdrop for any stone fruits, such as peaches, plums, or apricots.

Warm Berry Compote
with Vanilla Frozen Yogurt

SERVES 4

YOGURT

$^1/_2$ cup sugar

$^1/_2$ cup water

1 vanilla bean

2 cups plain yogurt

COMPOTE

1 cup quartered fresh strawberries

$^1/_2$ cup fresh raspberries

$^1/_2$ cup fresh blueberries

6 fresh basil leaves, cut into
thin strips (see note, page 24)

TO PREPARE THE YOGURT: Combine the sugar and water in a small saucepan. Split the vanilla bean lengthwise and, using the back of a knife, scrape the seeds into the pan. Add the pod and bring to a full boil. Remove from the heat and cool to room temperature. Combine $^1/_2$ cup of the sugar mixture and the yogurt in a small container and place in the freezer for 2 hours, or until completely frozen. Reserve the remaining sugar mixture.

Place the frozen yogurt in a food processor and pulse for 2 to 3 minutes, or until the mixture is smooth. Freeze the yogurt until ready to serve.

TO PREPARE THE COMPOTE: Cook the strawberries, raspberries, blueberries, and the remaining sugar mixture in a medium saucepan over medium heat for 3 to 4 minutes, or until hot. Add the basil, stir, and remove from the heat.

Spoon the warm compote into the center of each plate and top with a scoop of the frozen yogurt.

> This yogurt can also be frozen in an ice cream machine, but I wanted to show you an alternative method if you don't own one. This yogurt will not be as smooth as it would be if it were spun in a machine, but it will have the same great flavor.

tarts, pies, and pastries

178 | Fresh Strawberry Tarts with Basil Crème Fraîche

180 | Warm Apple-Date Tart with Honey-Caramel Sauce

182 | Cherry-Pecan Tart with Orange-Caramel Sauce

184 | Ginger–Chocolate Ganache Tart with Poached Pears

185 | Apple Crisp with Apple-Buttermilk Sherbet

187 | Chocolate Pecan Pie

188 | Lemon-Blueberry Meringue Tarts with Stewed Blueberries

190 | Two-Berry Linzertorte with Black Pepper Anglaise

192 | Peach Tarte Tatin with Gingered Yogurt Sauce

194 | Warm Peach Turnovers with Almond Ice Cream

Fresh Strawberry Tarts
with Basil Crème Fraîche

SERVES 6

DOUGH

1¼ cups flour

⅔ cup cold unsalted butter, chopped

2 tablespoons sugar

¾ teaspoon salt

1 egg yolk

3 tablespoons ice water

STRAWBERRIES

2 cups sliced fresh strawberries

¼ cup sugar

CRÈME FRAÎCHE

1 cup crème fraîche

1 tablespoon finely grated orange zest

4 fresh basil leaves, cut into thin strips (see note, page 24)

2 tablespoons sugar

TO PREPARE THE TART SHELLS: Using an electric mixer or by hand, combine the flour, butter, sugar, and salt in a large bowl until pebble-sized balls form. Combine the egg yolk and ice water in a small bowl, add to the flour mixture, and mix until the dough just comes together. Remove the dough from the bowl, pat into a disk, and cover with plastic wrap. Refrigerate for at least 1 hour.

Preheat the oven to 325°. On a floured surface, roll out the dough ⅛ inch thick and cut out 6 circles large enough to line a 3-inch-diameter by ½-inch-high tartlet ring. Place 6 tartlet rings on a parchment-lined baking sheet, and press a dough circle into each one, trimming any excess. (Alternatively, use an 8- or 9-inch tart pan.) Line the tarts with parchment paper and fill with pastry weights or dried beans to prevent the dough from bubbling or shrinking. Bake the tart shells for 15 minutes, or until golden brown. Cool the tart shells on the pan, and then carefully remove the tartlet rings, weights, and parchment.

MEANWHILE, PREPARE THE STRAWBERRIES: Place the strawberries in a medium bowl, toss with the sugar, and set aside for 30 minutes, or until the sugar is dissolved.

TO PREPARE THE CRÈME FRAÎCHE: Combine the crème fraîche, orange zest, basil, and sugar in a small bowl, mixing well.

TO PREPARE THE TARTS: Spread 2 tablespoons of the crème fraîche mixture in the bottom of each tart shell. Arrange some of the strawberries in each shell and top with crème fraîche.

> Traditional crème fraîche is unpasteurized 30 percent butterfat cream that has been allowed to ferment naturally. It has a nutty, faintly sour flavor and a smooth texture. Because nearly all dairy products in the United States must be pasteurized, here it is made with buttermilk and heavy cream. Crème fraîche is available in some grocery stores, but it is simple to make your own. Combine 1 cup heavy cream with 2 tablespoons buttermilk and let it sit at room temperature for 8 to 12 hours, or until it is very thick. Once it is thick, it can be refrigerated for up to 10 days.

Warm Apple-Date Tart
with Honey-Caramel Sauce

SERVES 8

TART SHELL

1¼ cups flour

⅔ cup cold unsalted butter, chopped

2 tablespoons sugar

¾ teaspoon salt

1 egg yolk

3 tablespoons ice water

CARAMEL SAUCE

1½ cups honey

½ cup heavy cream

¼ cup freshly squeezed lemon juice

2 cups pitted dates, halved lengthwise

¼ cup flour

3 Granny Smith apples, peeled, cored, and cut into ⅛-inch-thick slices

TO PREPARE THE TART SHELL: Using an electric mixer or by hand, combine the flour, butter, sugar, and salt in a large bowl until pebble-sized balls form. Combine the egg yolk and ice water in a small bowl, add to the flour mixture, and mix just until the dough comes together. Remove the dough from the bowl, pat into a disk, and cover with plastic wrap. Refrigerate for at least 1 hour.

Preheat the oven to 350°. On a floured surface, roll out the dough ⅛ inch thick, and then press it into a 9-inch tart pan, trimming any excess. Line the tart with parchment paper and fill with pastry weights or dried beans to prevent the dough from bubbling or shrinking. Bake for 15 to 20 minutes, or until light golden brown. Remove from the oven, let cool, and remove the weights and parchment. Leave the oven on.

MEANWHILE, PREPARE THE CARAMEL SAUCE: Bring the honey to a boil in a large saucepan over medium heat and cook for 10 minutes, or until dark golden brown. Remove from the heat and stir in the cream very slowly. Set aside.

TO PREPARE THE TART: Place 2 tablespoons of the lemon juice in a medium bowl, add the dates, and toss. Drain any excess lemon juice. Toss the dates with the flour, and then arrange them in a single layer in the bottom of the tart. Spoon one-third of the caramel sauce over the dates. Place the remaining 2 tablespoons lemon juice in a medium bowl, add the apples, and toss. Drain any excess lemon juice. Starting in the center, arrange the apple slices in a pinwheel pattern on top of the dates. Brush with one-third of the caramel sauce.

Return the tart to the oven and bake for 30 to 40 minutes, or until the apples are tender. Cool and then cut into 8 slices.

Place a slice of tart in the center of each plate and drizzle the remaining caramel sauce over the tart and around the plates.

> Caramelizing honey can be tricky, but the rich flavor that results is worth the effort. Honey splatters as it cooks, so use a large pan with high sides to keep from getting burned. When adding the cream, add a tiny bit at a time, or it will splatter out of control. The best tip for making this sauce is to wear oven mitts while cooking it.

Cherry-Pecan Tart with Orange-Caramel Sauce

SERVES 8

TART SHELL

1 cup flour

$^1/_3$ cup cold unsalted butter, chopped

$^1/_3$ cup granulated sugar

$^1/_8$ teaspoon salt

1 egg yolk

1 tablespoon plus 1 teaspoon heavy cream

FILLING

$^1/_2$ cup plus 2 tablespoons granulated sugar

$^1/_2$ cup firmly packed brown sugar

1 cup corn syrup

3 tablespoons unsalted butter

1 teaspoon pure vanilla extract

$^1/_4$ teaspoon salt

2 eggs plus 2 egg yolks

1 cup dried cherries

$1^1/_2$ cups (6 ounces) coarsely chopped pecans, toasted (see note, page 36)

TO PREPARE THE TART SHELL: Using an electric mixer or by hand, combine the flour, butter, sugar, and salt in a medium bowl until pebble-sized balls form. Combine the egg yolk and cream in a small bowl, add to the flour mixture, and mix just until the dough comes together. Remove the dough from the bowl, pat into a disk, and cover with plastic wrap. Refrigerate for at least 1 hour.

On a floured surface, roll out the dough $^1/_8$ inch thick, and then press it into an 8- or 9-inch tart pan. Refrigerate for 30 minutes, and trim away any excess dough.

TO PREPARE THE FILLING: Preheat the oven to 350°. Combine the granulated sugar, brown sugar, and corn syrup in a medium bowl. Brown the butter in a small sauté pan over medium heat until it is smoky and has a nutty aroma. Remove from the heat, immediately add to the sugar mixture, and stir to mix well. Add the vanilla and salt and mix thoroughly to combine. Allow the mixture to cool, and then add the eggs and egg yolks, stirring to combine.

TO PREPARE THE TART: Evenly distribute the cherries and pecans in the bottom of the tart shell and pour in the sugar mixture. Bake for 20 to 25 minutes, or until the dough is golden brown and the filling is bubbly. Remove from the oven, cool, and cut into 8 slices.

SAUCE

$1/2$ cup granulated sugar

$1/4$ cup water

$1/4$ cup freshly squeezed
orange juice

TO PREPARE THE SAUCE: While the tart is baking, cook the sugar and water in a small, heavy-bottomed sauté pan over medium heat for 10 minutes, or until deep golden brown and caramelized. Do not stir the sugar while it is over the heat, or it may crystallize.

Remove from the heat, add the orange juice, and stir to mix thoroughly. Cool to room temperature.

Place a slice of tart in the center of each plate and drizzle the sauce around the plates.

> When caramelizing sugar to make caramel sauce, resist the urge to stir it. Stirring can cause the sugar to crystallize. If it is heating unevenly, swirl the sugar in the pan a couple of times to even it out, but don't stir until it is off the heat. If it does crystallize, throw it away and start over.

Ginger–Chocolate Ganache Tart with Poached Pears

TART SHELL

6 tablespoons unsalted butter, at room temperature

$^1/_2$ cup sugar

1 egg

$^3/_4$ teaspoon pure vanilla extract

$^1/_2$ teaspoon salt

$^1/_3$ cup sifted unsweetened cocoa powder

$^3/_4$ cup flour

FILLING

12 ounces bittersweet chocolate, chopped

1 tablespoon unsalted butter

$1^3/_4$ cups heavy cream

$^1/_2$ cup peeled and chopped fresh ginger

$^1/_2$ cup preserved ginger (see page 6)

Unsweetened cocoa powder for dusting

PEARS

2 cups white wine

2 sticks cinnamon

8 black peppercorns

$^1/_2$ cup firmly packed brown sugar

4 small pears, peeled, halved, and cored

TO PREPARE THE TART SHELL: Using an electric mixer or by hand, cream the butter, sugar, egg, vanilla, and salt in a large bowl until smooth. Add the cocoa powder and mix well. Add the flour and mix until incorporated. Transfer the dough to a lightly floured work surface and shape it into a ball. Cover with plastic wrap and refrigerate for 1 hour.

Preheat the oven to 375°. On a floured surface, roll out the dough $^1/_8$ inch thick, and then press it into an 8- or 9-inch tart pan, trimming any excess. Prick the dough several times with a fork and bake for 15 to 20 minutes, or until light golden brown. Remove from the oven and cool completely.

TO MAKE THE FILLING: Place the chocolate and butter in a medium bowl. Bring the cream and fresh ginger to a boil in a medium saucepan over medium heat, strain the mixture through a fine-mesh sieve over the chocolate, and discard the ginger. Let the chocolate mixture stand for 3 minutes, and then whisk until smooth. Fold in the preserved ginger and pour the mixture into the tart shell. Refrigerate for 3 hours. Dust the tart with cocoa powder and cut into 8 slices.

TO PREPARE THE PEARS: Combine the wine, cinnamon sticks, peppercorns, and brown sugar in a medium saucepan. Add the pears and bring to a simmer over medium heat. Simmer for 15 minutes, or until the pears are tender.

Place a slice of the tart in the center of each plate, and top it with a poached pear half.

> This rich, intensely chocolate ganache also makes wonderful truffles. Prepare the ganache, pour into a bowl, and refrigerate. Once it has hardened, form the truffles by using a small scoop. Roll them in cocoa powder or dip in melted chocolate.

Apple Crisp with
Apple-Buttermilk Sherbet

SERVES 6

SHERBET

3/4 cup buttermilk

1 cup apple juice

1/2 cup simple syrup (see page 6)

1 1/2 tablespoons corn syrup

TOPPING

1/4 cup sugar

1/2 cup cold unsalted butter, cubed

1/2 cup flour

1/4 cup cornmeal

APPLE

1 1/2 cups peeled and diced Granny Smith apple

1 cup water

2 tablespoons freshly squeezed lemon juice

1/4 cup sugar

2 tablespoons crème fraîche

TO PREPARE THE SHERBET: Combine all of the ingredients for the sherbet in a medium bowl and refrigerate until chilled. Freeze in an ice cream machine and keep frozen until ready to use.

TO PREPARE THE TOPPING: Preheat the oven to 325°. Combine the sugar, butter, flour, and cornmeal with a fork or in a food processor until crumbly. Spread the mixture on a baking sheet and bake for 25 minutes, or until golden brown. Remove from the oven, cool slightly, and crumble into small pieces.

TO PREPARE THE APPLE: Cook the apple, water, lemon juice, and sugar in a medium sauté pan over medium heat, stirring continuously, for about 15 minutes, or until the water evaporates and the sugar begins to turn light golden brown and caramelize. Remove from the heat, add the creme fraîche, and mix thoroughly.

Place a 2 1/2-inch ring mold (or other similar-sized mold) in the center of each plate. Spoon the apple mixture into the molds and top with about 2 tablespoons of the topping mixture, pressing down firmly. Remove the mold and top with a scoop of the sherbet.

Many of the desserts we make at the restaurant use ring molds. Ring molds can be purchased in any gourmet kitchen shop, but, in most cases, a round, deep cookie cutter will do the trick.

Chocolate Pecan Pie

SERVES 8

PIE CRUST

1/2 cup cold unsalted
butter, chopped

4 ounces cold cream cheese,
cubed

4 ounces flour (about 3/4 cup)

FILLING

4 ounces bittersweet chocolate,
chopped

1/4 cup heavy cream

3 tablespoons unsalted butter

2 cups (8 ounces) pecans

5 tablespoons firmly packed
brown sugar

3 tablespoons granulated sugar

1/2 cup bourbon

3/4 cup corn syrup

1 vanilla bean

3 egg yolks

1 pint heavy cream

> The cream cheese dough
> used here is extremely flaky
> and rich. It is excellent in
> place of regular pie dough.

TO PREPARE THE PIE CRUST: Using an electric mixer or by hand, combine the butter, cream cheese, and flour in a large bowl until the dough just comes together (it should have visible streaks of cream cheese). Remove the dough from the bowl, pat into a disk, and cover in plastic wrap. Refrigerate for at least 1 hour.

On a floured surface, roll out the dough 1/8 inch thick, and then press it into an 8- or 9-inch pie pan, trimming any excess. Cover and refrigerate until ready to use.

MEANWHILE, PREPARE THE FILLING: Place the chocolate in a medium bowl. Place the cream and 1 tablespoon of the butter in a small saucepan and bring to a boil over medium heat. Pour the cream over the chocolate and let stand for 3 minutes. Whisk together until smooth and refrigerate until firm.

TO PREPARE THE PIE: Preheat the oven to 350°. Spread the chilled chocolate in the bottom of the prepared crust. Spread the pecans evenly over the chocolate. Combine the brown sugar, granulated sugar, bourbon, and corn syrup in a small bowl. Split the vanilla bean lengthwise and, using the back of a knife, scrape the seeds out into a small sauté pan. Add the remaining 2 tablespoons butter and cook over medium heat until the butter is dark brown and has a nutty aroma. Pour the browned butter over the sugar mixture and mix well. Add the egg yolks and mix well. Pour the mixture over the pecans, and bake the pie for 20 minutes, or until set. Remove from the oven and cool to room temperature.

Whip the cream into soft peaks. Cut the pie into 8 slices, place a piece on each plate, put a dollop of whipped cream next to each slice, and serve.

Lemon-Blueberry Meringue Tarts with Stewed Blueberries

SERVES 6

TART SHELLS

1¼ cups flour

⅔ cup cold unsalted butter, chopped

2 tablespoons sugar

¾ teaspoon salt

1 egg yolk

3 tablespoons ice water

CUSTARD FILLING

6 eggs

1 cup plus 1 tablespoon sugar

½ cup freshly squeezed lemon juice

¾ cup fresh blueberries

COMPOTE

¼ cup sugar

2 tablespoons water

1 cup fresh blueberries

TO PREPARE THE TART SHELLS: Using an electric mixer or by hand, combine the flour, butter, sugar, and salt in a large bowl until pebble-sized balls form. Combine the egg yolk and water in a small bowl, add to the flour mixture, and mix just until the dough comes together. Remove the dough from the bowl, pat into a disk, and cover with plastic wrap. Refrigerate for at least 1 hour.

Preheat the oven to 325°. On a floured surface, roll out the dough ⅛ inch thick and cut out 6 circles large enough to line a 3-inch-diameter by ½-inch-high tartlet ring. Place 6 tartlet rings on a parchment-lined baking sheet, and press a dough circle into each one, trimming any excess. (Alternatively, use an 8- or 9-inch tart pan.) Line the tarts with parchment paper and fill with pastry weights or dried beans to prevent the dough from bubbling or shrinking. Bake the tart shells for 15 minutes, or until golden brown. Remove from the oven and increase the oven temperature to 400°. Cool the tart shells on the pan, then carefully remove the tartlet rings, weights, and parchment.

MEANWHILE, PREPARE THE CUSTARD FILLING: Prepare a double boiler with barely simmering water. Separate 4 of the eggs and set aside the whites in a medium bowl. Combine the egg yolks, the remaining 2 whole eggs, the 1 cup sugar, and the lemon juice in the top of the double boiler. Stir continuously for 5 minutes, or until thickened. Strain through a fine-mesh sieve and set aside.

Whip the reserved egg whites with an electric mixer or by hand until frothy, add the remaining 1 tablespoon sugar, and whip until soft peaks form.

TO PREPARE THE TARTS: Stir the blueberries into the custard and spoon into the tart shells. Spoon the egg whites over the custard, covering the entire top of each tart. Return the tarts to the oven and bake for 8 to 10 minutes, or until lightly browned. Remove from the oven and cool to room temperature.

TO PREPARE THE COMPOTE: While the tarts are baking, cook the sugar and water in a small sauté pan over medium heat for 5 minutes, or until golden brown and caramelized. Do not stir the sugar while it is over the heat, or it may crystallize (see note, page 183). Remove from the heat and quickly stir in the blueberries. Return the pan to the heat and cook for 30 seconds, or until any hardened sugar is melted.

Spoon some of the warm compote onto the center of each plate and top with a tart.

Cooking blueberries in caramelized sugar can be tricky. If they cook too long, they will get mushy. The key is to move quickly. The process of adding the blueberries and melting any hardened sugar should take no more than 1 minute. If you are not serving the blueberries right away, transfer them to a bowl immediately, so the hot pan doesn't continue to cook them.

Two-Berry Linzertorte
with Black Pepper Anglaise

SERVES 8

TART SHELL

3/4 cup unsalted butter, at room temperature

1 cup confectioners' sugar

1 1/2 teaspoons grated lemon zest

1 tablespoon grated orange zest

3 egg yolks

1 2/3 cups flour

1 teaspoon baking powder

2 teaspoons ground cinnamon

1 teaspoon ground nutmeg

1/4 teaspoon salt

2 cups hazelnuts, toasted (see note, page 36), skinned, and ground

FILLING

1 1/2 cups quartered strawberries

1 1/2 cups fresh raspberries

1 1/2 tablespoons cornstarch

3 tablespoons granulated sugar

1 egg, lightly beaten

TO PREPARE THE TART SHELL: Using an electric mixer or by hand, cream the butter, confectioners' sugar, and lemon and orange zests in a large bowl until well mixed. Add the egg yolks and mix until just combined. Add the flour, baking powder, cinnamon, nutmeg, salt, and hazelnuts and continue mixing until just combined. Refrigerate the dough for several hours and then roll out between 2 sheets of parchment paper to about 1/8 inch thick. Press the dough into a 9-inch tart pan and trim off and reserve any excess. Cover with plastic wrap and refrigerate for 1 hour. Work the excess dough together, place in a pastry bag fitted with a flat tip, and set aside.

TO PREPARE THE FILLING: Toss together the strawberries, raspberries, cornstarch, and sugar in a medium bowl.

TO PREPARE THE LINZERTORTE: Distribute the berry mixture evenly in the tart shell. Pipe horizontal and vertical lines of the excess dough across the top of the tart to form a lattice design. Brush with the egg and refrigerate for 2 hours.

Preheat the oven to 350°. Bake the linzertorte for 25 minutes, or until golden brown. Remove from the oven, cool, and cut into 8 slices.

PEPPER ANGLAISE

3/4 cup plus 2 tablespoons heavy cream

1 tablespoon black pepper

2 egg yolks

1 tablespoon sugar

TO PREPARE THE PEPPER ANGLAISE: Bring the cream and black pepper to a boil in a medium saucepan over medium heat. Whisk together the egg yolks and sugar in a medium bowl and slowly whisk in some of the hot cream to temper the eggs. Pour the eggs into the cream and cook over medium heat for 2 to 3 minutes, or until the mixture coats the back of a spoon and steam rises from the surface. Just prior to serving, blend with a handheld blender (see note, page 152) or standard blender set on high speed until frothy.

Place a slice of tart in the center of each plate and drizzle the sauce over the tart and around the plates.

The linzertorte is a popular dessert that originated in Linz, Austria. I have adapted this recipe slightly from the traditional one, which calls for almonds in the dough and is spread with jam instead of whole fruit. But one thing is traditional about this torte: the sticky dough. Make sure it is completely chilled before rolling it; the colder it is, the easier it will be to handle. During warm weather you may even need to refrigerate the dough after rolling it, in order to remove the parchment paper.

Peach Tarte Tatin with Gingered Yogurt Sauce

SERVES 8

CRUST

¹/₂ cup cold unsalted butter, cut into chunks

4 ounces cold cream cheese, cubed

4 ounces flour (about ³/₄ cup)

FILLING

2 peaches, peeled, halved, and pitted

1 cup sugar

¹/₄ cup water

SAUCE

³/₄ cup plain yogurt

2 tablespoons juice from preserved ginger (see page 6)

TO PREPARE THE CRUST: Using an electric mixer or by hand, combine the butter, cream cheese, and flour in a large bowl until it just comes together (it should have visible streaks of cream cheese). Remove the dough from the bowl, pat into a disk, and cover in plastic wrap. Refrigerate for at least 1 hour.

On a floured surface, roll out the dough ¹/₄ inch thick and cut into 8 circles, each 2¹/₂ inches in diameter. Cover with plastic wrap and refrigerate until ready to use.

TO PREPARE THE FILLING: Cut two ¹/₄-inch-thick slices from each peach half. Lay out the peach slices and trim to form 2¹/₂-inch circles. Discard the remaining peaches.

Cook the sugar and water in a large, heavy-bottomed sauté pan over medium heat for 10 minutes, or until golden brown and caramelized. Do not stir the sugar while it is over heat, or it may crystallize (see note, page 183).

TO PREPARE THE TARTS: Preheat the oven to 350°. Wrap the bottoms of eight 2¹/₂-inch-diameter by 1¹/₂-inch-high ring molds (see note, page 185) in aluminum foil and place them on a baking sheet. Spoon some of the caramelized sugar into each ring mold and swirl to coat the bottom. Top with a circle of peach and then a circle of dough, and bake for 30 to 40 minutes, or until golden brown.

MEANWHILE, PREPARE THE SAUCE: Combine the yogurt and preserved ginger juice in a small bowl.

Remove the tarts from the oven, immediately invert onto serving plates, and remove the aluminum foil. Drizzle the sauce around the plates and serve warm.

In France, where tarte Tatin originated, the tart is called *tarte des desmoiselles Tatin,* which, literally translated, means "the tart of two unmarried women named Tatin." It was created by two sisters in the Loire Valley who made their living making these upside-down tarts with apples. The tart is also good with peaches (as I have used here) and with pineapple.

Warm Peach Turnovers with Almond Ice Cream

SERVES 6

ICE CREAM

2 cups heavy cream

1 cup ground almonds

4 egg yolks

6 tablespoons granulated sugar

CRUST

1/2 cup cold unsalted
butter, chopped

4 ounces cold cream cheese,
cubed

4 ounces flour (about 3/4 cup)

FILLING

1/2 cup granulated sugar

1/4 cup water

2 peaches, peeled and cut into
12 wedges each

2 tablespoons freshly squeezed
lemon juice

1/4 cup crème fraîche

1 egg, lightly beaten

Confectioners' sugar for dusting

TO PREPARE THE ICE CREAM: Fill a large bowl halfway with ice and cold water. Combine the cream and almonds in a medium saucepan, bring to a boil over high heat, and remove from the heat. Whisk together the egg yolks and sugar in a small bowl and slowly whisk in some of the hot cream mixture to temper the eggs. Pour the egg mixture into the cream and cook over medium heat for 2 to 3 minutes, or until the mixture coats the back of a spoon and steam rises from the surface. Strain into a bowl through a fine-mesh sieve and cool in the ice water bath, stirring occasionally, until chilled. Freeze in an ice cream machine and keep frozen until ready to use.

TO PREPARE THE CRUST: Using an electric mixer or by hand, combine the butter, cream cheese, and flour in a large bowl until it just comes together (it should have visible streaks of cream cheese). Remove the dough from the bowl, pat into a disk, and cover in plastic wrap. Refrigerate for at least 1 hour.

On a floured surface, roll out the dough 1/8 inch thick. Cut into 12 2 1/2-inch squares, cover, and refrigerate until ready to use.

TO PREPARE THE FILLING: Cook the sugar and water in a medium sauté pan for 10 minutes, or until golden brown and caramelized. Do not stir the sugar while it is over the heat, or it may crystallize (see note, page 183). Add the lemon juice and crème fraîche and stir well. Gently stir the peaches into the sugar mixture, remove from the heat, and cool in the pan. Using a slotted spoon, remove the peaches from the pan, reserving the sauce.

TO PREPARE THE TURNOVERS: Preheat the oven to 350°. Place 2 peach wedges on each dough square. Fold the dough over the peaches to form a triangle. Brush the very tip of the dough with the egg and press firmly to seal. Place the turnovers on a baking sheet. Brush the tops of the turnovers with the egg and bake for 30 minutes, or until golden brown. Cool slightly and dust with confectioners' sugar.

Place 2 turnovers back-to-back on each plate and top with a small scoop of almond ice cream. Drizzle the sauce over the turnovers and around the plate.

These turnovers are fantastic when served warm, but they could be made ahead and served at room temperature with warm sauce. Plums, figs, and apples would also be delicious.

cakes, custards, and puddings

197 | German Chocolate Cake with Toasted Pecan Sauce

199 | Molasses Spice Cake with Caramelized Apples

200 | Key Lime Pudding Cake with Dried-Fruit Compote

202 | Caramelized Pineapple-Polenta Cake with Caramel Ice Cream

204 | Chocolate-Praline Bread Pudding with Cinnamon Cream

206 | Cinnamon-Cranberry Bread Pudding with Vanilla Anglaise

207 | Jasmine Rice Pudding with Lemon-Caramel Sauce

209 | Plum-Pistachio Trifle

210 | Vanilla Couscous Custard with Strawberry–Red Flame Raisin Compote

211 | Vanilla Crème Brûlée with Chocolate Sauce

212 | Sweet Potato–Brown Rice Pudding with Sherry Wine Vinegar–Caramel Sauce

213 | Baked Apples with Sweet Curry Mascarpone Cream

German Chocolate Cake
with Toasted Pecan Sauce

SERVES 8

CAKE

6 tablespoons unsweetened
cocoa powder

1/4 cup flour

1/4 teaspoon salt

12 eggs, separated

1 1/2 cups sugar

1 tablespoon pure vanilla extract

FILLING

4 cups heavy cream

2 3/4 cups shredded fresh
coconut, toasted

1/2 cup freshly squeezed
orange juice

3/4 cup sugar

1/3 cup corn syrup

SAUCE

1 cup half-and-half

1/3 cup ground toasted pecans,
plus 1/2 cup coarsely chopped
toasted pecans (see note, page 36)

1 egg yolk

1/2 cup sugar

TO PREPARE THE CAKE: Preheat the oven to 350°. Line 2 8- or 9-inch round baking pans with parchment paper and butter the paper and the sides of the pans. Sift together the cocoa, flour, and salt into a medium bowl. Whip the egg yolks in a large bowl until light in color. Add the sugar to the egg yolks 2 tablespoons at a time, mixing well between additions. Add the vanilla and mix well. Add the dry ingredients and mix just until combined.

Using an electric mixer or by hand, whip the egg whites to stiff peaks. Stir one-quarter of the whites into the batter to lighten the mixture. Fold the remaining egg whites into the batter in 3 separate additions to avoid breaking down the egg whites. Pour the batter into the baking pans and bake for 30 to 35 minutes, or until the cake springs back when lightly pressed and starts to pull away from the sides of the pan. Remove from the oven and cool slightly in the pans. Invert the cakes onto a cooling rack, carefully remove the parchment paper, and cool completely.

MEANWHILE, PREPARE THE FILLING: Cook the cream, 1 cup of the toasted coconut, the orange juice, sugar, and corn syrup over medium-low heat for 30 to 40 minutes, or until reduced to about 2 cups. Fill a large bowl halfway with ice and cold water. Strain the cream mixture into a large bowl through a fine-mesh sieve and chill over the ice water bath, stirring occasionally. Remove the bowl from the ice water bath and fold in the remaining 1 3/4 cups coconut.

continued

TO ASSEMBLE THE CAKE: Using a long, thin knife, slice each cake in half horizontally to form 4 layers in all. Place 1 cake layer in the center of a large plate. Spread one-quarter of the filling over the entire layer and top with another layer of cake. Continue layering the remaining cake layers and filling.

TO PREPARE THE SAUCE: Bring the half-and-half and ground pecans to a boil in a medium saucepan over medium heat. Whisk together the egg yolk and sugar in a small bowl, and slowly whisk in some of the hot cream to temper the egg. Pour the egg mixture into the cream and cook over medium heat for 2 to 3 minutes, or until the mixture coats the back of a spoon and steam rises from the surface. Strain through a fine-mesh sieve.

Place a slice of cake in the center of each plate. Spoon the warm sauce around the cake, and sprinkle the pecan pieces over the sauce.

Fresh coconut is a must for this recipe. It is less sweet and tastes so much better than packaged coconut. For this recipe, you will need 2 average-sized coconuts. Pierce 3 holes in one end of each coconut. Drain the liquid and place the coconuts in a 400° oven for 20 minutes, or until the shells crack. Separate the coconut meat from the shells, and peel the dark outer skin from the meat. Shred the coconut with a handheld grater or in a food processor, place on a baking sheet, and toast in a preheated 300° oven for 10 minutes, or until golden brown.

Molasses Spice Cake
with Caramelized Apples

SERVES 9

CAKE

3/4 cup milk

2 tablespoons brandy

1 1/2 teaspoons rice wine vinegar

2 cups flour

1 1/2 teaspoons baking soda

1/4 teaspoon salt

1 teaspoon ground cinnamon

1/8 teaspoon ground cloves

1/2 cup unsalted butter, at room temperature

1/3 cup sugar

2 eggs

3/4 cup light molasses

APPLES

2 cups sugar

1/2 cup water

3 apples, peeled, cored, and cut into 1/8-inch-thick slices

1/4 cup preserved ginger (see page 6)

1 tablespoon freshly squeezed lemon juice

TO PREPARE THE CAKE: Preheat the oven to 350°. Line a 9-inch square pan with parchment paper and butter and flour the bottom and sides of the pan.

Combine the milk, brandy, and vinegar in a small bowl. Sift together the flour, baking soda, salt, cinnamon, and cloves into a medium bowl. Using an electric mixer or by hand, cream the butter and sugar in a large bowl until light and fluffy. Add the eggs and continue beating until they are fully incorporated. Add the molasses and mix well. Alternately add the dry ingredients and the milk mixture to the batter, mixing well after each addition. Pour the batter into the prepared pan and bake for 25 to 30 minutes, or until a toothpick inserted in the center of the cake comes out clean. Remove from the oven and cool to room temperature.

MEANWHILE, PREPARE THE APPLES: While the cake is baking, cook the sugar and water in a medium, heavy-bottomed sauté pan over medium heat for 15 minutes, or until the sugar is golden brown and caramelized. Do not stir the sugar while it is over the heat, or it may crystallize (see note, page 183). Add the apples, ginger, and lemon juice and simmer over medium heat, stirring frequently, for 3 minutes.

Cut the cake into 3-inch squares. Place a piece of cake in the center of each plate, top with some of the apples, and spoon the sauce from the apples around the plate.

> Molasses is a by-product of sugar refining. There are three types—light, dark, and blackstrap—resulting from the first, second, and third boiling of the sugarcane. The first boiling produces the lightest, sweetest, mildest-flavored molasses.

Key Lime Pudding Cake
with Dried-Fruit Compote

SERVES 12

CAKE

¼ cup unsalted butter,
at room temperature

1 cup plus 2 tablespoons sugar

Pinch of salt

3 tablespoons grated key lime zest

6 egg yolks

6 tablespoons flour

¼ cup freshly squeezed
key lime juice

2 cups milk

8 egg whites

COMPOTE

2 cups mixed dried fruits (such as
cherries, apricots, and cranberries)

1 cup simple syrup (see page 6)

4 key lime leaves, sliced very thinly

TO PREPARE THE PUDDING CAKE: Preheat the oven to 325°.
Line a 9- by 13-inch pan with plastic wrap. Using an electric
mixer or by hand, cream the butter, sugar, salt, and lime zest
in a large bowl. Add the egg yolks one at a time, mixing well
after each addition. Add the flour and mix well. Add the lime
juice and milk and mix well. Beat the egg whites to stiff peaks
and fold into the batter. Pour the batter into the prepared pan
and place the pan in a large roasting pan. Pour in enough water
to reach halfway up the sides of the cake pan (see note, page
206). Bake in the water bath for 35 to 45 minutes, or until
light brown and firm. Remove from the oven, remove the pan
from the water bath, cool slightly, and refrigerate until completely chilled. Invert the cake onto a baking sheet, remove
the plastic wrap, and cut into 12 3-inch squares just prior to
serving.

TO PREPARE THE COMPOTE: Cook the dried fruits and simple
syrup in a small saucepan over medium-low heat for 10 minutes, or until the fruits are soft.

Place a slice of pudding cake in the center of each plate
and spoon the compote around the cake. Sprinkle the key lime
leaves over each plate and serve.

> This cake will separate into a pudding layer and a cake layer
> as it cooks. There are three things to watch for when making
> it: (1) Don't overmix when you add the egg whites; it is better
> to have some white streaks than to deflate the egg whites.
> (2) Watch the cake carefully toward the end of the cooking time.
> Remove it from the oven when it is just beginning to become
> golden brown and is firm to the touch. (3) Make sure the cake is
> well chilled before inverting it, or it may break apart.

Caramelized Pineapple-Polenta Cake with Caramel Ice Cream

SERVES 9

ICE CREAM

2 cups heavy cream

1 teaspoon finely grated lime zest

6 tablespoons sugar

4 egg yolks

3 tablespoons freshly squeezed lime juice

CAKE

$3/4$ cup unsalted butter, at room temperature

$1^3/4$ cups sugar

3 eggs plus 6 egg yolks

$3/4$ cup plus 1 tablespoon flour

$1/2$ cup plus 2 tablespoons uncooked polenta

$3/4$ teaspoon baking powder

$1/2$ teaspoon salt

$1/4$ cup water

9 $1/8$-inch-thick fresh pineapple slices, cored

TO PREPARE THE ICE CREAM: Fill a large bowl halfway with ice and cold water. Bring the cream and lime zest to a boil in a large saucepan over medium heat, remove from the heat, and cover. Cook the sugar in a medium saucepan over medium heat for 5 to 7 minutes, or until golden brown and caramelized. Do not stir the sugar while it is over the heat, or it may crystallize (see note, page 183). Add the hot cream to the sugar and stir until completely combined. Whisk the egg yolks, then slowly whisk in some of the hot cream to temper the eggs. Pour the egg mixture into the cream and cook for 2 to 3 minutes, or until the mixture coats the back of a spoon and steam rises from the surface. Strain into a medium bowl through a fine-mesh sieve and place in the ice water bath, stirring occasionally, until chilled. Add the lime juice to the cooled cream mixture and freeze in an ice cream machine. Keep frozen until ready to use.

TO PREPARE THE CAKE: Using an electric mixer or by hand, cream the butter and 1 cup of the sugar in a large bowl. Add the eggs and egg yolks one at a time, mixing thoroughly after each addition. Combine the flour, polenta, baking powder, and salt in a separate bowl and add to the batter, mixing completely.

Preheat the oven to 350°. Lightly oil the sides of an 8- or 9-inch baking pan. Cook the remaining 3/4 cup sugar and the water in a small, heavy-bottomed sauté pan over medium heat for 10 minutes, or until golden brown and caramelized. Again, do not stir the sugar, or it may crystallize. Pour the sugar into the baking pan and swirl around to coat the bottom of the pan. Arrange the pineapple rings in the baking pan in a single layer and refrigerate for 5 minutes. Spoon the batter into the pan and bake for 20 minutes, or until the cake springs back when pressed lightly in the center. Remove from the oven and invert the warm cake onto a large plate. Cut the cake into 9 pieces.

Place a piece of warm cake in the center of each plate and top with a scoop of the ice cream.

This cake can be prepared ahead up to the point of baking and then refrigerated for 2 or 3 hours, or until you are ready to bake it. The cake must be baked at the last moment to ensure that the caramelized sugar is hot and the cake can be turned upside down without sticking to the pan.

Chocolate-Praline Bread Pudding
with Cinnamon Cream

SERVES 9

PRALINE

³/₄ cup granulated sugar

¹/₄ cup water

³/₄ cup pecans, toasted
(see note, page 36)

PUDDING

3 cups heavy cream

3 eggs plus 3 egg yolks

¹/₂ cup granulated sugar

9 ounces bittersweet
chocolate, chopped

6 cups cubed day-old bread

CREAM

¹/₂ cup heavy cream

¹/₂ teaspoon ground cinnamon

2 tablespoons confectioners' sugar

TO PREPARE THE PRALINE: Oil a baking sheet or line it with a silicone baking mat. Cook the sugar and water in a medium sauté pan over medium heat for 10 minutes, or until golden brown and caramelized. Do not stir the sugar while it is over the heat, or it may crystallize (see note, page 183). Add the pecans and stir until incorporated. Immediately pour the hot praline onto the prepared baking sheet. Let cool and then break into small pieces.

TO PREPARE THE PUDDING: Preheat the oven to 350°. Butter a 9-inch square pan. Bring the cream to a boil in a medium saucepan. Whisk together the eggs, egg yolks, and sugar in a medium bowl. Slowly whisk in some of the hot cream to temper the eggs, and then pour the egg mixture into the cream and cook over medium heat for 2 to 3 minutes, or until the sugar is dissolved. Place one-third of the chocolate in a medium bowl and pour in the cream mixture. Whisk until the chocolate is completely melted. Place the bread cubes in a large bowl and pour in the chocolate-cream mixture. Allow the bread to soak, turning occasionally, until all of the liquid is absorbed. Fold in the remaining chocolate and 1 cup of the praline. Spoon the mixture into the prepared pan and place the pan in a large roasting pan. Pour in enough water to reach halfway up the sides of the cake pan (see note, page 206). Bake in the water bath for 45 minutes, or until a knife inserted in the center comes out clean. Remove from the oven, remove the pan from the water bath, and cool for 10 minutes. Cut into 3-inch squares.

TO PREPARE THE CREAM: Using an electric mixer or by hand, whip the cream and the cinnamon in a medium bowl until soft peaks just begin to form. Add the confectioners' sugar and mix until just incorporated.

Place a piece of bread pudding in the center of each plate. Spoon the cinnamon cream over the pudding and around the plate and sprinkle with some of the praline.

Silicone is the ultimate nonstick surface. Silicone baking mats are relatively inexpensive and can be found in many gourmet cooking shops.

Cinnamon-Cranberry Bread Pudding
with Vanilla Anglaise

SERVES 9

PUDDING

3 cups heavy cream

2 sticks cinnamon

3 eggs plus 3 egg yolks

1/2 cup sugar

6 cups cubed day-old bread

3/4 cup dried cranberries

3/4 cup coarsely chopped walnuts, toasted (see note, page 36)

VANILLA ANGLAISE

1 cup heavy cream

1 vanilla bean

2 egg yolks

4 teaspoons sugar

> Custards should always be cooked in a water bath to even out the oven heat and prevent the eggs from curdling. Set the pan with the custard in a larger pan, place it in the oven, and then pour about 1 inch of water into the larger pan.

TO PREPARE THE PUDDING: Preheat the oven to 350°. Butter a 9-inch square baking pan.

Place the cream and cinnamon sticks in a large saucepan over medium heat and bring to a boil. Whisk together the eggs, egg yolks, and sugar in a small bowl and slowly whisk in some of the hot cream to temper the eggs. Pour the egg mixture into the cream and cook for 2 to 3 minutes, or until the mixture coats the back of a spoon and steam rises from the surface. Place the bread in a large bowl and pour in the cream mixture. Allow the bread to soak, turning occasionally, until all of the liquid is absorbed. Fold in the cranberries and walnuts and spoon the mixture into the prepared pan. Place the pan in a large roasting pan. Pour in enough water to reach halfway up the sides of the cake pan. Bake in the water bath for 45 minutes, or until a knife inserted in the center comes out clean. Remove from the oven, remove the pan from the water bath, and cool for 10 minutes. Cut into 3-inch squares.

TO PREPARE THE ANGLAISE: While the pudding cools, place the cream in a small saucepan. Split the vanilla bean lengthwise and, using the back of a knife, scrape the seeds out into the cream. Add the pod to the cream and bring to a boil. Whisk together the egg yolks and sugar in a medium bowl and slowly whisk in the cream. Return the mixture to the saucepan and cook over medium heat, stirring continuously, for 2 minutes, or until the sauce coats the back of a spoon and steam rises from the surface. Strain into a bowl through a fine-mesh sieve and keep warm.

Place a piece of the pudding in the center of each plate and spoon the anglaise over the pudding and around the plate.

Jasmine Rice Pudding
with Lemon-Caramel Sauce

SERVES 9

PUDDING

1 cup jasmine rice (see note, page 116)

1 tablespoon minced lemon zest

2 cups water

3/4 cup sugar

2 cups milk

2 eggs plus 2 egg yolks

1 1/2 cups heavy cream

SAUCE

1 cup sugar

1/4 cup water

1/4 cup freshly squeezed lemon juice, warmed

It takes a little more work to prepare the jasmine rice in the style of a risotto, but it results in a much creamier pudding. Here, I flavor the pudding with lemon zest, but almost any type of spice would also work well.

TO PREPARE THE PUDDING: Simmer the rice, lemon zest, water, and 1/2 cup of the sugar in a large saucepan over medium heat, stirring frequently, for 20 minutes, or until all of the liquid is absorbed. Add 1/2 cup of the milk and simmer until all of the liquid is absorbed. Repeat with the remaining milk and remove from the heat.

Preheat the oven to 350°. Whisk together the eggs, egg yolks, and remaining 1/4 cup sugar in a large mixing bowl. Bring the cream to a boil in a medium saucepan over medium heat and then slowly whisk some of the hot cream into the egg mixture to temper the eggs. Pour the egg mixture into the cream and cook for 2 to 3 minutes, or until the mixture coats the back of a spoon and steam rises from the surface. Pour the mixture over the rice and stir well. Pour the pudding into a 9-inch square pan and place the pan in a large roasting pan filled with enough water to reach halfway up the sides of the pudding pan (see note, page 206). Bake in the water bath for 35 to 45 minutes, or until the pudding is set. Remove from the oven, remove the pudding pan from the water bath, and cool slightly. Refrigerate until chilled.

TO PREPARE THE SAUCE: Cook the sugar and water in a small sauté pan over medium heat for 10 minutes, or until golden brown and caramelized. Do not stir the sugar while it is over the heat, or it may crystallize (see note, page 183). Remove the pan from the heat and slowly stir in the lemon juice until completely incorporated. Return the pan to the heat to dissolve any hardened sugar and then remove from the heat and cool to room temperature.

Cut the rice pudding into 3-inch squares. Place a piece of pudding in the center of each plate and drizzle the sauce over the pudding and around the plate.

Plum-Pistachio Trifle

SERVES 12

CAKE

2 tablespoons milk

1 tablespoon unsalted butter

6 tablespoons sugar

2 eggs plus 1 egg yolk

6 tablespoons flour

1/2 teaspoon baking powder

FILLING

20 red plums, peeled, pitted, and sliced

1 1/4 cups simple syrup (see page 6)

1/2 cup water

1/2 cup heavy cream

1 cup mascarpone cheese (see note, page 213)

3/4 cup chopped pistachios, toasted (see note, page 36)

> A trifle dish is traditionally a large, deep clear glass bowl with straight sides. Any type of bowl will work, but clear glass is best to show off the beautiful layers in this dessert.

TO PREPARE THE CAKE: Preheat the oven to 400°. Line a 9- by 13-inch pan with parchment paper and butter the sides of the pan.

Heat the milk and butter in a small saucepan over low heat until warm. Prepare a double boiler with barely simmering water. Whisk together the sugar, eggs, and egg yolk in the top of the double boiler and cook for 5 minutes, or until the sugar is dissolved. Transfer the sugar mixture to a large bowl and whip with an electric mixer or by hand until tripled in volume. Fold in the flour and baking powder until combined. Add the warm milk and fold in until just combined. Spread the batter into the prepared pan and bake for 10 minutes, or until light golden brown. Remove from the oven and let cool. Cut into 2- by 3-inch pieces.

TO PREPARE THE FILLING: Place the plums, simple syrup, and water in a large saucepan and cook over medium heat for 15 minutes, or until the plums are tender. Remove from the heat and cool.

Place the cream in a medium bowl and whip by hand or with an electric mixer until soft peaks form. Add the mascarpone and whip until stiff peaks form. Fold in about one-third of the plums.

Spoon one-third of the plums into the bottom of a trifle dish and top with one-third of the mascarpone mixture. Sprinkle with one-third of the pistachios and arrange the cake pieces to form a complete layer over the pistachios. Repeat the process, finishing with a final layer of filling topped by pistachios (there should be 3 layers of filling and 2 layers of cake.)

Vanilla Couscous Custard with Strawberry–Red Flame Raisin Compote

SERVES 6

CUSTARD

1 tablespoon powdered unflavored gelatin

$^1/_4$ cup water

1 cup heavy cream

6 tablespoons milk

$^1/_2$ cup sugar

1 cup cooked couscous

COMPOTE

$^1/_2$ cup simple syrup (see page 6)

$^3/_4$ cup Red Flame raisins

$^3/_4$ cup sliced fresh strawberries

TO PREPARE THE CUSTARD: Fill a large bowl halfway with ice and cold water. Combine the gelatin with the water in a small bowl. Cook the cream, milk, and sugar in a medium saucepan over medium heat for 5 minutes, or until the sugar is dissolved. Add the gelatin to the cream, and stir until completely combined. Transfer the cream to a large bowl and cool in the ice water bath, stirring occasionally, until chilled.

Fold together the couscous and the cream mixture and refrigerate for 1 hour, or until the mixture has thickened enough to keep the couscous evenly distributed in the custard. Spoon into 6 lightly oiled ring molds $2^1/_2$ inches in diameter by $1^1/_2$ inches high or into small custard dishes, and refrigerate.

TO PREPARE THE COMPOTE: Cook the simple syrup and raisins in a small saucepan over medium-low heat for 10 minutes. Add the strawberries, toss until coated, and remove from the heat.

Place a custard-filled ring mold in the center of each plate. Remove the mold and spoon the compote around the custard.

> Red Flame raisins have the same flavor as regular raisins, but they are about the size of a dried cherry. I use them here because of their size, but regular raisins would work just as well.

Vanilla Crème Brûlée
with Chocolate Sauce

SERVES 6

¹/₄ cup simple syrup (see page 6)

¹/₂ cup unsweetened cocoa powder

2 eggs plus 2 egg yolks

5 tablespoons sugar

1¹/₂ cups heavy cream

¹/₂ cup milk

1 vanilla bean

Sugar for dusting

TO PREPARE THE CRÈME BRÛLÉE: Preheat the oven to 300°. Fill a large bowl halfway with ice and cold water. Combine the simple syrup and cocoa in a small bowl. Place a spoonful of the sauce in the bottom of six 4- or 5-inch diameter ramekins and place in the freezer until ready to use.

Whisk together the eggs, egg yolks, and sugar in a small bowl until smooth. Place the cream and milk in a small saucepan. Split the vanilla bean lengthwise and, using the back of a knife, scrape the seeds out into the cream mixture. Bring to a boil over medium heat. Slowly whisk the hot cream mixture into the eggs and mix well. Strain into a medium bowl through a fine-mesh sieve and cool in the ice water bath.

Pour the custard mixture into the ramekins with the chocolate and place the ramekins in a large roasting pan. Pour in enough water to reach halfway up the sides of the ramekins (see note, page 206). Bake in the water bath for 35 to 45 minutes, or until the custard jiggles slightly when shaken. Remove from the oven, remove the custards from the water bath, and cool slightly. Refrigerate until chilled.

Sprinkle a dusting of sugar over the top of each custard and place in the center of each plate. Using a small hand-held blow torch, slowly caramelize the sugar until it is golden brown and serve.

> If you don't have a small blow torch, the sugar can be caramelized under a broiler. Place the oven rack as close to the broiler as possible and watch the custards carefully; they will need to be rotated often to keep the sugar from burning.

Sweet Potato–Brown Rice Pudding with Sherry Wine Vinegar–Caramel Sauce

SERVES 9

RICE

3/4 cup brown rice

1 1/2 cups water

1 cup milk

1/4 cup granulated sugar

1 tablespoon finely grated orange zest

PUDDING

1 large sweet potato, peeled and diced

1/4 cup firmly packed brown sugar

2 tablespoons unsalted butter, chopped

1 1/2 cups heavy cream

2 tablespoons bourbon

3 eggs

1/2 cup granulated sugar

1/8 teaspoon ground cinnamon

Dash of ground nutmeg

2 cups cubed day-old bread

SAUCE

1 cup granulated sugar

1/4 cup water

1 cup sherry wine vinegar

TO COOK THE RICE: Combine the rice, water, milk, sugar, and orange zest in a saucepan. Cover and cook over medium-low heat for 50 to 60 minutes, or until tender. Cool to room temperature.

MEANWHILE, PREPARE THE PUDDING: Preheat the oven to 350°. Place the sweet potato in a bowl and toss with the brown sugar and butter. Place on a baking sheet and bake for 30 minutes, or until tender. Remove from the oven; leave the oven on.

Lightly oil a 9-inch square pan. In a small bowl, whisk together the cream, bourbon, eggs, sugar, cinnamon, and nutmeg. Place the bread cubes in a large bowl and pour the cream mixture over it. Refrigerate for 30 minutes.

Fold the rice and sweet potatoes into the bread mixture. Pour into the prepared pan, and place the pan in a large roasting pan. Pour in enough water to reach halfway up the sides of the pudding pan (see note, page 206). Bake in the water bath for 35 to 40 minutes, or until set. Remove from the oven, remove the pudding pan from the water bath, cool slightly, and cut into 3-inch squares.

TO PREPARE THE SAUCE: Cook the sugar and water in a small saucepan over medium heat for 5 minutes, or until light brown. Do not stir the sugar while it is over the heat, or it may crystallize (see note, page 183). Add the vinegar and cook, stirring occasionally, for 10 minutes, or until deep golden brown.

Place a piece of pudding in the center of each plate and drizzle some of the sauce over the pudding and around the plate.

Making caramel sauce with vinegar is a good way to tone down the sweetness of a dessert.

Baked Apples with
Sweet Curry Mascarpone Cream

SERVES 6

APPLES

1 cup chopped dates

1/2 cup chopped walnuts

1 tablespoon freshly squeezed lemon juice

2 tablespoons brown sugar

6 McIntosh apples, cored

CREAM

1/2 cup mascarpone cheese

2 tablespoons simple syrup (see page 6)

1/2 teaspoon curry powder (see note, page 30)

TO PREPARE THE APPLES: Preheat the oven to 350°. Toss the dates, walnuts, and lemon juice together in a small bowl. Add the brown sugar and mix well. Place the apples on a baking sheet and press the date mixture into the centers. Bake for 30 to 40 minutes, or until the apples are slightly soft.

TO PREPARE THE CREAM: Place all of the ingredients for the cream in a small bowl and mix well.

Place a warm baked apple in the center of each plate and spoon the mascarpone cream over the apples and around the plates.

> Mascarpone is a soft, creamy, mild-flavored cheese made in Switzerland and Italy. It is available in most grocery stores. Unfortunately, there is really no good substitute for mascarpone. If it is unavailable, however, for this recipe, you could whip some heavy cream to soft peaks and mix in a little confectioners' sugar and the curry powder.

index

Aioli, Roasted Red Bell Pepper, 23

Almonds
  Almond-Crusted Chicken Breast with Spinach and Citrus Vinaigrette, 110
  Almond Ice Cream, 194
  Almond Shortbread, 169–70

Anchovy Vinaigrette, 67

Apples
  Apple Crisp with Apple-Buttermilk Sherbet, 185
  Baked Apples with Sweet Curry Mascarpone Cream, 213
  Cold-Poached Salmon with Shaved Fennel and Apple Salad, 90
  Molasses Spice Cake with Caramelized Apples, 199
  Warm Apple Cider Soup with Crispy Apple Turnovers, 168
  Warm Apple-Date Tart with Honey-Caramel Sauce, 180–81
  Whole Roasted Duck with Red Wine–Braised Apples, 119
  Yellow Squash and Granny Smith Apple Soup with Preserved Squash, 48

Apricots
  Apricot-Curry Chicken and Quinoa Salad, 60–62
  Apricot-Curry Sauce, 30
  Chilled Apricot Soup with Vanilla Bean Ice Cream and Almond Shortbread, 169–70
  Chilled Pork and Wild Rice Salad with Citrus Vinaigrette, 59

Artichokes, Israeli Couscous Salad with Spinach, Kalamata Olives, and, 65

Asian Pear, Cantaloupe, and Mango Salad with Key Lime–Vanilla Bean Vinaigrette, 70

Asparagus
  Chilled Asparagus and Basil Soup with Goat Cheese, 40
  Chilled Orzo, Asparagus, Chicken, and Goat Cheese Salad, 63
  Grilled Beef Tenderloin with Asparagus and Roasted Red Onion Vinaigrette, 130
  Steamed Sea Bass with Yukon Gold Potato Purée and Asparagus, 82

Bacon
  Bacon and Caramelized Onion Tart, 33
  Bacon-Sherry Vinaigrette, 137
  Grilled Bacon-Wrapped Beef Tenderloin with Wild Mushroom Risotto, 126–27
  Lentil and Bacon Soup, 53
  Sweet Corn and Shrimp Chowder, 45

Barley-Mushroom Soup, 49

Basil Crème Fraîche, 178–79

Beans
  Ginger-Braised Spareribs with Cilantro-Scented Navy Beans, 136
  Lobster Tail with Horseradish Potatoes and Haricots Verts, 96
  Shaved Fennel and Haricots Verts Salad with Mustard Vinaigrette, 72
  Three Bean and Potato Salad with Horseradish Vinaigrette, 69

Beef
  Cardamom Beef Stew with Potatoes, Celery Root, and Parsnips, 128
  Grilled Bacon-Wrapped Beef Tenderloin with Wild Mushroom Risotto, 126–27
  Grilled Beef Tenderloin and Blue Cheese Salad, 57
  Grilled Beef Tenderloin with Asparagus and Roasted Red Onion Vinaigrette, 130
  Grilled Strip Loin Steaks with Rosemary-Potato Purée and Meat Jus, 129
  Grilled Tamari Beef with Shiitake Mushrooms and Daikon, 31
  Meat Stock, 3
  Meat Stock Reduction, 4
  Poached Beef Tenderloin with Fingerling Potatoes, Brussels Sprouts, and Beef Broth, 134
  Red Wine–Braised Short Ribs with Garlic Mashed Potatoes, 123–24
  Sliced Flank Steak Salad with Grilled Radicchio and Roasted Shallot Vinaigrette, 58
  Stuffed Beef Tenderloin with Whole Wheat Couscous and Black Olive Vinaigrette, 132–33
  Yukon Gold Potato and Braised Oxtail Tarts, 147–48

Beet, Pickled, and Endive Salad with Goat Cheese and Walnuts, 68

Bell peppers
  Apricot-Curry Chicken and Quinoa Salad, 60–62
  Grilled Vegetable Salad with Anchovy Vinaigrette, 67
  Roasted Bell Pepper, 5
  Roasted Red Bell Pepper Aioli, 23
  Spring Rolls with Sweet and Sour Yogurt Sauce, 34
  Sweet Curry–Red Bell Pepper Sauce, 20
  Vegetable "Lasagna" with Roasted Garlic Broth, 158

Black Olive Vinaigrette, 132

Blueberries
  Lemon-Blueberry Meringue Tarts with Stewed Blueberries, 188–89
  Warm Berry Compote with Vanilla Frozen Yogurt, 175

Blue cheese
  Chicken Roulade with Blue Cheese, Black Walnuts, and Spinach and Basmati Rice, 107
  Grilled Beef Tenderloin and Blue Cheese Salad, 57
  Maytag Blue Cheese Croutons, 51

Bok choy
  Cilantro-Crusted Tuna Loin with Bok Choy and Lemon-Sesame Vinaigrette, 78
  Panko-and-Ginger-Crusted Chicken with Stir-Fried Vegetables and Sweet and Sour Mustard Sauce, 115
  Ponzu-Marinated Scallops with Daikon and Bok Choy, 93

Broccoli Rabe, Olive Oil–Poached Cod with Roasted Tomatoes and, 85

Brown Butter–Citrus Vinaigrette, 156

Brussels Sprouts, Poached Beef Tenderloin with Fingerling Potatoes, Beef Broth, and, 134

Butternut Squash Ravioli with Brown Butter–Citrus Vinaigrette, 156–57

Cabbage
  Sautéed Veal Chops with Braised Juniper Berry–Infused Red Cabbage, 135
  Spring Rolls with Sweet and Sour Yogurt Sauce, 34

Cantaloupe, Mango, and Asian Pear Salad with Key Lime–Vanilla Bean Vinaigrette, 70

Cardamom Beef Stew with Potatoes, Celery Root, and Parsnips, 128

Celery Root, Cardamom Beef Stew with Potatoes, Parsnips, and, 128

Champagne Granité, Poached Peaches with, 171

Cheese. See individual cheeses

Cherries
  Cherry-Pecan Tart with Orange-Caramel Sauce, 182–83
  Warm Bing Cherries with White Chocolate–Bing Cherry Sorbet, 174

Chicken
  Almond-Crusted Chicken Breast with Spinach and Citrus Vinaigrette, 110
  Apricot-Curry Chicken and Quinoa Salad, 60–62
  Chicken Liver Croutons, 52
  Chicken Roulade with Blue Cheese, Black Walnuts, and Spinach and Basmati Rice, 107
  Chicken Stock, 4
  Chilled Orzo, Asparagus, Chicken, and Goat Cheese Salad, 63
  Crispy Chicken Wontons with Apricot-Curry Sauce, 30
  Curry-Braised Chicken and Potato Tarts, 28–29
  Egg Drop Soup with Ginger-Braised Chicken, 44
  Orange Blossom Honey–Glazed Chicken with Roasted Sweet Potato Purée, 109

Panko-and-Ginger-Crusted Chicken with Stir-Fried Vegetables and Sweet and Sour Mustard Sauce, 115

Pumpkin Soup with Chicken and Ginger-Braised Leeks, 46

Thyme-and-Mustard-Marinated Grilled Chicken with Horseradish Potato Salad, 108

Chocolate
Chocolate Pecan Pie, 187
Chocolate-Praline Bread Pudding with Cinnamon Cream, 204–5
German Chocolate Cake with Toasted Pecan Sauce, 197–98
Ginger–Chocolate Ganache Tart with Poached Pears, 184
Vanilla Crème Brûlée with Chocolate Sauce, 211

Chowder, Sweet Corn and Shrimp, 45

Cider Soup, Warm Apple, with Crispy Apple Turnovers, 168

Cilantro-Crusted Tuna Loin with Bok Choy and Lemon-Sesame Vinaigrette, 78

Cinnamon-Cranberry Bread Pudding with Vanilla Anglaise, 206

Corn
Lobster and Sweet Corn Ravioli with Sweet Corn Broth, 24
Sweet Corn and Shrimp Chowder, 45

Cornish Hens, Cumin-Garlic-Rubbed, with Potato-Parmesan Pavé, 113–14

Couscous
Israeli Couscous Salad with Spinach, Artichokes, and Kalamata Olives, 65
Stuffed Beef Tenderloin with Whole Wheat Couscous and Black Olive Vinaigrette, 132–33
Vanilla Couscous Custard with Strawberry–Red Flame Raisin Compote, 210

Crab Cakes with Sweet Curry–Red Bell Pepper Sauce, 20

Crackers, Whole Wheat–Cumin, 25

Cranberry-Cinnamon Bread Pudding with Vanilla Anglaise, 206

Cream cheese
Chocolate Pecan Pie, 187
Peach Tarte Tatin with Gingered Yogurt Sauce, 192–93
Warm Peach Turnovers with Almond Ice Cream, 194–95

Crème Brûlée, Vanilla, with Chocolate Sauce, 211

Crème fraîche, Basil, 178–79

Crisp, Apple, with Apple-Buttermilk Sherbet, 185

Cucumbers
Apricot-Curry Chicken and Quinoa Salad, 60–62
Chilled Cucumber Soup with Kimchi, 43
Pickled Cucumber Vinaigrette, 56

Cumin-Garlic-Rubbed Cornish Hens with Potato-Parmesan Pavé, 113–14

Curry Oil, 6

Daikon, Grilled Tamari Beef with Shiitake Mushrooms and, 31
Ponzu-Marinated Scallops with Daikon and Bok Choy, 93

Date-Apple Tart, Warm, with Honey-Caramel Sauce, 180–81

Duck
Duck Breast–Spinach Salad with Ginger-Soy Vinaigrette, 64
Sautéed Duck Breasts with Swiss Chard, Ginger-Braised Celery, and Orange Vinaigrette, 117
Whole Roasted Duck with Red Wine–Braised Apples, 119

Egg Drop Soup with Ginger-Braised Chicken, 44

Eggplant
Grilled Salmon Steaks with Marinated Tomatoes and Eggplant, 91
Grilled Tuna Steak with Quinoa and Roasted Shallot Vinaigrette, 79–80
Grilled Vegetable Salad with Anchovy Vinaigrette, 67
Ratatouille, 138
Sautéed Sea Bass with Roasted White Eggplant and Black Olive Purées, 81

Fennel
Cold-Poached Salmon with Shaved Fennel and Apple Salad, 90
Shaved Fennel and Haricots Verts Salad with Mustard Vinaigrette, 72

Fettuccine and Spinach in Saffron-Mussel Broth, 104

Filo dough
Warm Apple Cider Soup with Crispy Apple Turnovers, 168

Fish
Cilantro-Crusted Tuna Loin with Bok Choy and Lemon-Sesame Vinaigrette, 78
Cold-Poached Salmon with Shaved Fennel and Apple Salad, 90
Grilled Catfish with Yellow Tomato Sauce and Scallions, 86
Grilled Salmon Steaks with Marinated Tomatoes and Eggplant, 91
Grilled Tuna Steak with Quinoa and Roasted Shallot Vinaigrette, 79–80
Herb-Crusted Halibut with Roasted Potatoes and Shiitake Mushroom Sauce, 102
Olive Oil–Poached Cod with Roasted Tomatoes and Broccoli Rabe, 85
Peppered Tuna with Wild Mushroom Ragout, 76
Sautéed Catfish with Caramelized Onion Risotto, 87
Sautéed Sea Bass with Roasted White Eggplant and Black Olive Purées, 81
Sautéed Snapper with Caramelized Onion–Strewn Grits and Red Wine Pan Sauce, 92
Sautéed Sweet and Sour Cod with Oyster Mushrooms and Somen Noodles, 83
Seared Tuna with Wasabi Sauce on Whole Wheat–Cumin Crackers, 25
Slow-Roasted Salmon with Garlic and Thyme Risotto, 88
Smoked Salmon and Herb Salad with Pickled Cucumber Vinaigrette, 56
Smoked Salmon and Potato Salad with Scallion-Citrus Vinaigrette, 55
Smoked Salmon Tartare with Horseradish Cream, 26
Steamed Sea Bass with Yukon Gold Potato Purée and Asparagus, 82

Garlic
Garlic and Thyme Risotto, 88
Garlic Mashed Potatoes, 123–24
Roasted Garlic, 5
Roasted Garlic Broth, 158
Roasted Garlic Soup with Chicken Liver Croutons, 52
Warm Tomato and Roasted Garlic Salad, 103

German Chocolate Cake with Toasted Pecan Sauce, 197–98

Ginger
Egg Drop Soup with Ginger-Braised Chicken, 44
Ginger-Braised Spareribs with Cilantro-Scented Navy Beans, 136
Ginger–Chocolate Ganache Tart with Poached Pears, 184
Gingered Yogurt Sauce, 192–93
Ginger-Soy Vinaigrette, 64
Molasses Spice Cake with Caramelized Apples, 199
Preserved Ginger, 6
Pumpkin Soup with Chicken and Ginger-Braised Leeks, 46

Gnocchi, Potato, with Oven-Roasted Tomatoes, Pearl Onions, and Goat Cheese, 162–63

Goat cheese
Chilled Asparagus and Basil Soup with Goat Cheese, 40
Chilled Orzo, Asparagus, Chicken, and Goat Cheese Salad, 63
Goat Cheese and Basil Ravioli with Tomato Water, 154
Goat Cheese–Stuffed Cherry Tomatoes, 36
Kalamata Olive and Goat Cheese Tapenade, 35
Pickled Beet and Endive Salad with Goat Cheese and Walnuts, 68
Potato Gnocchi with Oven-Roasted Tomatoes, Pearl Onions, and Goat Cheese, 162–63

Goose, Peppercorn-and-Thyme-Roasted, 120

Grapefruit
Chilled Ginger-Melon Soup with Citrus Granité, 167

Grits, Caramelized Onion–Strewn, 92

Hazelnuts
  Two-Berry Linzertorte with Black Pepper Anglaise, 190–91
Honey
  Honey-Caramel Sauce, 180
  Orange Blossom Honey–Glazed Chicken with Roasted Sweet Potato Purée, 109
Horseradish
  Horseradish Cream, 26
  Horseradish Potatoes, 96
  Horseradish Potato Salad, 108
  Horseradish Vinaigrette, 69
  Panko-and-Horseradish-Crusted Shrimp with Miso Broth, 101

Ice cream
  Almond Ice Cream, 194
  Caramel Ice Cream, 202–3
  Vanilla Bean Ice Cream, 169
Israeli Couscous Salad with Spinach, Artichokes, and Kalamata Olives, 65

Jasmine Rice Pudding with Lemon-Caramel Sauce, 207

Kalamata Olive and Goat Cheese Tapenade, 35
Kimchi, Chilled Cucumber Soup with, 43

Lamb
  Meat Stock, 3
  Meat Stock Reduction, 4
  Peppered Lamb Loin with Mustard Spaetzle and Thyme Reduction, 145–46
  Rack of Lamb with Crispy Polenta and Mustard Sauce, 142–44
  Whole Roasted Vidalia Onions Stuffed with Braised Lamb Shank and Roasted Parsnips, 140–41
"Lasagna," Vegetable, with Roasted Garlic Broth, 158
Leeks
  Braised Leek Soup with Sautéed Oyster Mushrooms, 50
  Open-Faced Wild Mushroom Tarts with Braised Leeks and Red Wine Emulsion, 151–52
  Panko-and-Ginger-Crusted Chicken with Stir-Fried Vegetables and Sweet and Sour Mustard Sauce, 115
  Pumpkin Soup with Chicken and Ginger-Braised Leeks, 46
  Spring Rolls with Sweet and Sour Yogurt Sauce, 34
Lemongrass Sorbet, Chilled Peach Soup with, 172
Lemons
  Chilled Ginger-Melon Soup with Citrus Granité, 167
  Lemon-Blueberry Meringue Tarts with Stewed Blueberries, 188–89
  Lemon-Caramel Sauce, 207
  Lemon-Sesame Vinaigrette, 78

Lentil and Bacon Soup, 53
Limes
  Key Lime Pudding Cake with Dried Fruit Compote, 200
  Key Lime–Vanilla Bean Vinaigrette, 70
Linzertorte, Two-Berry, with Black Pepper Anglaise, 190–91
Lobster
  Lobster and Sweet Corn Ravioli with Sweet Corn Broth, 24
  Lobster Tail with Horseradish Potatoes and Haricots Verts, 96

Mangoes
  Cantaloupe, Mango, and Asian Pear Salad with Key Lime–Vanilla Bean Vinaigrette, 70
  Spicy Fruit Salsa, 19
Mascarpone cheese
  Baked Apples with Sweet Curry Mascarpone Cream, 213
  Plum-Pistachio Trifle, 209
Maytag Blue Cheese Croutons, 51
Meat Stock, 3
Meat Stock Reduction, 4
Melons
  Cantaloupe, Mango, and Asian Pear Salad with Key Lime–Vanilla Bean Vinaigrette, 70
  Chilled Ginger-Melon Soup with Citrus Granité, 167
Molasses Spice Cake with Caramelized Apples, 199
Mozzarella cheese
  Vegetable "Lasagna" with Roasted Garlic Broth, 158
Mushrooms
  Braised Leek Soup with Sautéed Oyster Mushrooms, 50
  Duck Breast–Spinach Salad with Ginger-Soy Vinaigrette, 64
  Grilled Bacon-Wrapped Beef Tenderloin with Wild Mushroom Risotto, 126–27
  Grilled Tamari Beef with Shiitake Mushrooms and Daikon, 31
  Herb-Crusted Halibut with Roasted Potatoes and Shiitake Mushroom Sauce, 102
  Mushroom-Barley Soup, 49
  Mushroom Broth, 49
  Open-Faced Wild Mushroom Tarts with Braised Leeks and Red Wine Emulsion, 151–52
  Peppered Tuna with Wild Mushroom Ragout, 76
  Roasted Mushrooms, 5
  Sautéed Sea Scallops with Wild Mushroom Stew, 100
  Sautéed Sweet and Sour Cod with Oyster Mushrooms and Somen Noodles, 83
  Whole Roasted Tomatoes with Wild Mushroom–Strewn Quinoa, 160–61
Mustard Sauce, 142, 144
Mustard Vinaigrette, 72

Noodles. See *Pasta and noodles*
Nuts, toasting, 36. See also *individual nuts*

Oils
  Curry Oil, 6
  Olive Oil–Poached Cod with Roasted Tomatoes and Broccoli Rabe, 85
Olives
  Black Olive Vinaigrette, 132
  Israeli Couscous Salad with Spinach, Artichokes, and Kalamata Olives, 65
  Kalamata Olive and Goat Cheese Tapenade, 35
  Sautéed Sea Bass with Roasted White Eggplant and Black Olive Purées, 81
Onions
  Bacon and Caramelized Onion Tart, 33
  Caramelized Onion–Strewn Grits, 92
  Grilled Scallop and Red Onion Brochettes, 95
  Potato Gnocchi with Oven-Roasted Tomatoes, Pearl Onions, and Goat Cheese, 162–63
  Roasted Red Onion Vinaigrette, 130
  Sautéed Catfish with Caramelized Onion Risotto, 87
  Tiny Red Potatoes Stuffed with Caramelized Onions, Golden Raisins, and Walnuts, 38
  Tomato Risotto with Caramelized Onion Purée, 153
  Vidalia Onion Soup with Wild Rice and Maytag Blue Cheese Croutons, 51
  Whole Roasted Vidalia Onions Stuffed with Braised Lamb Shank and Roasted Parsnips, 140–41
Orange Blossom Honey–Glazed Chicken with Roasted Sweet Potato Purée, 109
Oranges
  Almond-Crusted Chicken Breast with Spinach and Citrus Vinaigrette, 110
  Brown Butter–Citrus Vinaigrette, 156
  Chilled Ginger-Melon Soup with Citrus Granité, 167
  Orange-Caramel Sauce, 182–83
  Orange Vinaigrette, 117
  Scallion-Citrus Vinaigrette, 55
Oxtail Tarts, Yukon Gold Potato and Braised, 147–48

Papayas
  Spicy Fruit Salsa, 19
Parsnips
  Cardamom Beef Stew with Potatoes, Celery Root, and Parsnips, 128
  Whole Roasted Vidalia Onions Stuffed with Braised Lamb Shank and Roasted Parsnips, 140–41
Pasta and noodles
  Chilled Orzo, Asparagus, Chicken, and Goat Cheese Salad, 63
  Fettuccine and Spinach in Saffron-Mussel Broth, 104
  Goat Cheese and Basil Ravioli with Tomato Water, 154

HOME COOKING WITH CHARLIE TROTTER

Grilled Shrimp and Vegetables with Linguine, 99

Mustard Spaetzle, 145

Sautéed Sweet and Sour Cod with Oyster Mushrooms and Somen Noodles, 83

Peaches

Chilled Peach Soup with Lemongrass Sorbet, 172

Peach Tarte Tatin with Gingered Yogurt Sauce, 192–93

Poached Peaches with Champagne Granité, 171

Warm Peach Turnovers with Almond Ice Cream, 194–95

Pea Risotto, Spring, with Spicy Herb Sauce, 164

Pears

Ginger–Chocolate Ganache Tart with Poached Pears, 184

Pickled Beet and Endive Salad with Goat Cheese and Walnuts, 68

Pecans

Cherry-Pecan Tart with Orange-Caramel Sauce, 182–83

Chocolate Pecan Pie, 187

Chocolate-Praline Bread Pudding with Cinnamon Cream, 204–5

Toasted Pecan Sauce, 197–98

Pepper

Pepper Anglaise, 191

Peppercorn-and-Thyme-Roasted Goose, 120

Peppered Lamb Loin with Mustard Spaetzle and Thyme Reduction, 145–46

Peppered Tuna with Wild Mushroom Ragout, 76

Pickling Juice, 6

Pie, Chocolate Pecan, 187

Pineapple

Caramelized Pineapple-Polenta Cake with Caramel Ice Cream, 202–3

Spicy Fruit Salsa, 19

Plum-Pistachio Trifle, 209

Polenta

Caramelized Pineapple-Polenta Cake with Caramel Ice Cream, 202–3

Rack of Lamb with Crispy Polenta and Mustard Sauce, 142–44

Ponzu-Marinated Scallops with Daikon and Bok Choy, 93

Pork

Chilled Pork and Wild Rice Salad with Citrus Vinaigrette, 59

Ginger-Braised Spareribs with Cilantro-Scented Navy Beans, 136

Herb-Crusted Pork Tenderloin with Roasted Yukon Gold Potatoes and Bacon-Sherry Vinaigrette, 137

Sautéed Pork Chops with Ratatouille, 138

Potatoes

Cardamom Beef Stew with Potatoes, Celery Root, and Parsnips, 128

Curry-Braised Chicken and Potato Tarts, 28–29

Garlic Mashed Potatoes, 123–24

Grilled Strip Loin Steaks with Rosemary-Potato Purée and Meat Jus, 129

Herb-Crusted Halibut with Roasted Potatoes and Shiitake Mushroom Sauce, 102

Herb-Crusted Pork Tenderloin with Roasted Yukon Gold Potatoes and Bacon-Sherry Vinaigrette, 137

Horseradish Potatoes, 96

Horseradish Potato Salad, 108

Poached Beef Tenderloin with Fingerling Potatoes, Brussels Sprouts, and Beef Broth, 134

Potato Gnocchi with Oven-Roasted Tomatoes, Pearl Onions, and Goat Cheese, 162–63

Potato-Parmesan Pavé, 113–14

Smoked Salmon and Potato Salad with Scallion-Citrus Vinaigrette, 55

Steamed Sea Bass with Yukon Gold Potato Purée and Asparagus, 82

Sweet Corn and Shrimp Chowder, 45

Three Bean and Potato Salad with Horseradish Vinaigrette, 69

Tiny Red Potatoes Stuffed with Caramelized Onions, Golden Raisins, and Walnuts, 38

Vegetable "Lasagna" with Roasted Garlic Broth, 158

Yukon Gold Potato and Braised Oxtail Tarts, 147–48

Pumpkin Soup with Chicken and Ginger-Braised Leeks, 46

Quinoa

Apricot-Curry Chicken and Quinoa Salad, 60–62

Grilled Tuna Steak with Quinoa and Roasted Shallot Vinaigrette, 79–80

Whole Roasted Tomatoes with Wild Mushroom–Strewn Quinoa, 160–61

Radicchio, Grilled, Sliced Flank Steak Salad with Roasted Shallot Vinaigrette and, 58

Raisins

Crispy Chicken Wontons with Apricot-Curry Sauce, 30

Tiny Red Potatoes Stuffed with Caramelized Onions, Golden Raisins, and Walnuts, 38

Vanilla Couscous Custard with Strawberry–Red Flame Raisin Compote, 210

Raspberries

Two-Berry Linzertorte with Black Pepper Anglaise, 190–91

Warm Berry Compote with Vanilla Frozen Yogurt, 175

Ratatouille, Sautéed Pork Chops with, 138

Ravioli

Butternut Squash Ravioli with Brown Butter–Citrus Vinaigrette, 156–57

Goat Cheese and Basil Ravioli with Tomato Water, 154

Lobster and Sweet Corn Ravioli with Sweet Corn Broth, 24

Rice

Chicken Roulade with Blue Cheese, Black Walnuts, and Spinach and Basmati Rice, 107

Grilled Bacon-Wrapped Beef Tenderloin with Wild Mushroom Risotto, 126–27

Jasmine Rice Pudding with Lemon-Caramel Sauce, 207

Sautéed Catfish with Caramelized Onion Risotto, 87

Shrimp Maki Rolls with Roasted Red Bell Pepper Aioli, 23

Slow-Roasted Salmon with Garlic and Thyme Risotto, 88

Spring Pea Risotto with Spicy Herb Sauce, 164

Sweet Potato–Brown Rice Pudding with Sherry Wine Vinegar–Caramel Sauce, 212

Tamari-and-Ginger-Roasted Turkey with Lemon-Ginger Jasmine Rice, 116

Tomato Risotto with Caramelized Onion Purée, 153

Risotto

Caramelized Onion Risotto, 87

Garlic and Thyme Risotto, 88

Spring Pea Risotto with Spicy Herb Sauce, 164

Tomato Risotto with Caramelized Onion Purée, 153

Wild Mushroom Risotto, 126–27

Saffron-Mussel Broth, Fettuccine and Spinach in, 104

Sauces and salsas

Apricot-Curry Sauce, 30

Gingered Yogurt Sauce, 192–93

Honey-Caramel Sauce, 180

Lemon-Caramel Sauce, 207

Mustard Sauce, 142, 144

Orange-Caramel Sauce, 182–83

Pepper Anglaise, 191

Sherry Wine Vinegar–Caramel Sauce, 212

Shiitake Mushroom Sauce, 102

Spicy Fruit Salsa, 19

Spicy Herb Sauce, 164

Sweet and Sour Mustard Sauce, 115

Sweet and Sour Yogurt Sauce, 34

Sweet Curry–Red Bell Pepper Sauce, 20

Toasted Pecan Sauce, 197–98

Vanilla Anglaise, 206

Wasabi Sauce, 25

Scallion-Citrus Vinaigrette, 55

Scallops

Grilled Scallop and Red Onion Brochettes, 95

Ponzu-Marinated Scallops with Daikon and Bok Choy, 93

Sautéed Sea Scallops with Wild Mushroom Stew, 100

Shallot Vinaigrette, Roasted, 58, 79

Sherbet, Apple-Buttermilk, 185

Shortbread, Almond, 169–70

Shrimp
  Grilled Shrimp and Vegetables with Linguine, 99
  Panko-and-Horseradish-Crusted Shrimp with Miso Broth, 101
  Shrimp Maki Rolls with Roasted Red Bell Pepper Aioli, 23
  Shrimp with Spicy Fruit Salsa, 19
  Sweet Corn and Shrimp Chowder, 45
Spaetzle, Mustard, 145
Spinach
  Almond-Crusted Chicken Breast with Spinach and Citrus Vinaigrette, 110
  Butternut Squash Ravioli with Brown Butter–Citrus Vinaigrette, 156–57
  Chicken Roulade with Blue Cheese, Black Walnuts, and Spinach and Basmati Rice, 107
  Duck Breast–Spinach Salad with Ginger-Soy Vinaigrette, 64
  Fettuccine and Spinach in Saffron-Mussel Broth, 104
  Grilled Beef Tenderloin and Blue Cheese Salad, 57
  Israeli Couscous Salad with Spinach, Artichokes, and Kalamata Olives, 65
Spring Pea Risotto with Spicy Herb Sauce, 164
Spring Rolls with Sweet and Sour Yogurt Sauce, 34
Squash
  Butternut Squash Ravioli with Brown Butter–Citrus Vinaigrette, 156–57
  Grilled Shrimp and Vegetables with Linguine, 99
  Grilled Vegetable Salad with Anchovy Vinaigrette, 67
  Ratatouille, 138
  Vegetable "Lasagna" with Roasted Garlic Broth, 158
  Yellow Squash and Granny Smith Apple Soup with Preserved Squash, 48
Stocks
  Chicken Stock, 4
  Meat Stock, 3
  Meat Stock Reduction, 4
  Vegetable Stock, 4
Strawberries
  Fresh Strawberry Tarts with Basil Crème Fraîche, 178–79
  Two-Berry Linzertorte with Black Pepper Anglaise, 190–91
  Vanilla Couscous Custard with Strawberry–Red Flame Raisin Compote, 210
  Warm Berry Compote with Vanilla Frozen Yogurt, 175
Sweet potatoes
  Orange Blossom Honey–Glazed Chicken with Roasted Sweet Potato Purée, 109
  Sweet Potato–Brown Rice Pudding with Sherry Wine Vinegar–Caramel Sauce, 212

Swiss Chard, Sautéed Duck Breasts with Ginger-Braised Celery, Orange Vinaigrette, and, 117
Syrup, Simple, 6
Tamari
  Grilled Tamari Beef with Shiitake Mushrooms and Daikon, 31
  Tamari-and-Ginger-Roasted Turkey with Lemon-Ginger Jasmine Rice, 116
Tapenade, Kalamata Olive and Goat Cheese, 35
Thyme-and-Mustard-Marinated Grilled Chicken with Horseradish Potato Salad, 108
Tomatoes
  Chilled Fresh Tomato Soup, 41
  Goat Cheese and Basil Ravioli with Tomato Water, 154
  Goat Cheese–Stuffed Cherry Tomatoes, 36
  Grilled Catfish with Yellow Tomato Sauce and Scallions, 86
  Grilled Halibut with Warm Tomato and Roasted Garlic Salad, 103
  Grilled Salmon Steaks with Marinated Tomatoes and Eggplant, 91
  Grilled Shrimp and Vegetables with Linguine, 99
  Olive Oil–Poached Cod with Roasted Tomatoes and Broccoli Rabe, 85
  Potato Gnocchi with Oven-Roasted Tomatoes, Pearl Onions, and Goat Cheese, 162–63
  Ratatouille, Sautéed Pork Chops with,138
  Tomato Risotto with Caramelized Onion Purée, 153
  Whole Roasted Tomatoes with Wild Mushroom–Strewn Quinoa, 160–61
Trifle, Plum-Pistachio, 209
Turkey, Tamari-and-Ginger-Roasted, with Lemon-Ginger Jasmine Rice, 116
Vanilla
  Vanilla Anglaise, 206
  Vanilla Bean Ice Cream, 169
  Vanilla Couscous Custard with Strawberry–Red Flame Raisin Compote, 210
  Vanilla Crème Brûlée with Chocolate Sauce, 211
  Vanilla Frozen Yogurt, 175
Veal
  Meat Stock, 3
  Meat Stock Reduction, 4
  Sautéed Veal Chops with Braised Juniper Berry–Infused Red Cabbage, 135
Vegetables. See also *individual vegetables*
  Grilled Shrimp and Vegetables with Linguine, 99
  Grilled Vegetable Salad with Anchovy Vinaigrette, 67
  Panko-and-Ginger-Crusted Chicken with Stir-Fried Vegetables and Sweet and Sour Mustard Sauce, 115

Vegetable "Lasagna" with Roasted Garlic Broth, 158
Vegetable Stock, 4
Vidalia Onion Soup with Wild Rice and Maytag Blue Cheese Croutons, 51
Walnuts
  Chicken Roulade with Blue Cheese, Black Walnuts, and Spinach and Basmati Rice, 107
  Chilled Pork and Wild Rice Salad with Citrus Vinaigrette, 59
  Pickled Beet and Endive Salad with Goat Cheese and Walnuts, 68
  Tiny Red Potatoes Stuffed with Caramelized Onions, Golden Raisins, and Walnuts, 38
Wasabi Sauce, 25
White Chocolate–Bing Cherry Sorbet, 174
Wild rice
  Chilled Pork and Wild Rice Salad with Citrus Vinaigrette, 59
  Vidalia Onion Soup with Wild Rice and Maytag Blue Cheese Croutons, 51
Wine
  Open-Faced Wild Mushroom Tarts with Braised Leeks and Red Wine Emulsion, 151–52
  Poached Peaches with Champagne Granité, 171
  Red Wine–Braised Short Ribs with Garlic Mashed Potatoes, 123–24
  Whole Roasted Duck with Red Wine–Braised Apples, 119
Wonton skins
  Butternut Squash Ravioli with Brown Butter–Citrus Vinaigrette, 156–57
  Crispy Chicken Wontons with Apricot-Curry Sauce, 30
  Lobster and Sweet Corn Ravioli with Sweet Corn Broth, 24
Yellow Squash and Granny Smith Apple Soup with Preserved Squash, 48
Yogurt
  Gingered Yogurt Sauce, 192–93
  Sweet and Sour Yogurt Sauce, 34
  Warm Berry Compote with Vanilla Frozen Yogurt, 175
Yukon Gold Potato and Braised Oxtail Tarts, 147–48
Zucchini
  Grilled Shrimp and Vegetables with Linguine, 99
  Grilled Vegetable Salad with Anchovy Vinaigrette, 67
  Ratatouille, Sautéed Pork Chops with,138
  Vegetable "Lasagna" with Roasted Garlic Broth, 158